**Concept developed by**
Caroline Clissold and Cherri Moseley

**Year 5 Author Team**
Caroline Clissold, Linda Glithro,
Steph King

The Publishers would like to thank the following for permission to reproduce copyright material.

Photo credits
Page 11: Kids shoes © Courtney. Licensed under CC BY 2.0; Page 25: Petrol station board (c)
Intelligent Car Leasing. Licensed under CC BY 2.0; page 46: The Pentagon. Licensed under
public domain via Wikimedia Commons; Pylon © Ewan Munro; Giraffe © Daniel Ramirez.
Licensed under CC BY 2.0; page 57: Surface of Mars © NASA; page 58: Stadium scoreboard
© Michael Barera. Licensed under CC BY 2.0; page 59: Big Ben. Licensed under public domain
via Wikimedia Commons; page 70: Checking bags in © Jeremyfoo. Licensed under CC BY 2.0;
page 81: Food label. Licensed under public domain under CC BY 2.0; page 94: Football players
© Jon Candy. Licensed under CC BY 2.0; page 106: Three zebras © Ralf Kayser. Licensed
under CC BY 2.0; page 141: The Baby Gap Store Canada © BargainMoose. Licensed under
CC BY 2.0; page 153: Wrapped presents © Liz West. Licensed under CC BY 2.0; page 177:
Ancient city of Carthage. Licensed under public domain via Wikimedia Commons

Acknowledgements
The reasoning skills on page 6 are based on John Mason's work on mathematical powers. See
Mason, J. and Johnston-Wilder, S. (Eds.) (2004). Learners powers. *Fundamental constructs in
Mathematics Education*. London: Routledge Falmer. 115-142.

Every effort has been made to trace all copyright holders, but if any have been inadvertently
overlooked, the Publishers will be pleased to make the necessary arrangements at the first
opportunity.
Although every effort has been made to ensure that website addresses are correct at time
of going to press, Rising Stars cannot be held responsible for the content of any website
mentioned in this book. It is sometimes possible to find a relocated web page by typing in the
address of the home page for a website in the URL window of your browser.

Hachette UK's policy is to use papers that are natural, renewable and recyclable products and
made from wood grown in sustainable forests. The logging and manufacturing processes are
expected to conform to the environmental regulations of the country of origin.

ISBN: 978 1 78339 526 2
Text, design and layout © Rising Stars UK Ltd 2015
First published in 2015 by
Rising Stars UK Ltd, part of  Hodder Education,
An Hachette UK Company
Carmelite House
50 Victoria Embankment
London EC4Y 0DZ
www.risingstars-uk.com
Authors: Caroline Clissold, Linda Glithro, Steph King

Programme Consultants: Caroline Clissold, Cherri Moseley, Paul Broadbent
Publishers: Fiona Lazenby and Alexandra Riley
Editorial: Jane Carr, Sarah Chappelow, Lynette James, Shannon Keenlyside,
Jackie Mace, Jane Morgan
Project manager: Sue Walton
Series and character design: Steve Evans
Illustrations by Steve Evans

Cover design: Steve Evans and Words & Pictures
Printed by Liberduplex, Barcelona
A catalogue record for this title is available from the British Library.

# Contents

# Introduction

Hello, I'm Amy. Welcome to *Rising Stars Mathematics!*

Look at the pictures at the beginning of the unit. Think about the mathematics you can see in the world around you.

Talk about the questions with your friends. Do you agree on the answers?

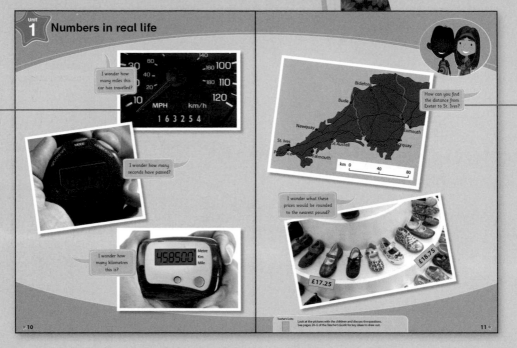

Read what Amy and Theo say. Can you spot if they have made a mistake?

Read the text and look at the diagrams to learn new maths skills. Your teacher will explain them.

Do these activities to practise what you have learnt. Write the answers in your exercise book.

These questions will help you explore and investigate maths. You will need to think about them carefully.

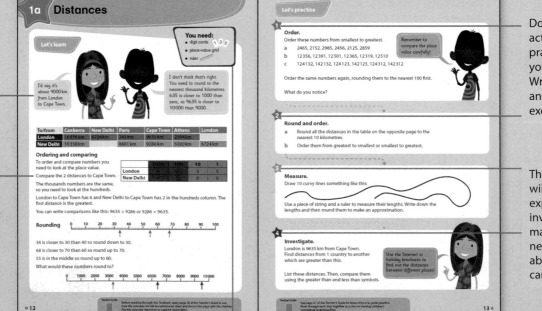

Use these items to help you. Make sure you have everything you need.

And I'm Theo. We'll help you as you learn with this book!

Play the game at the end of the unit to practise what you have learnt.

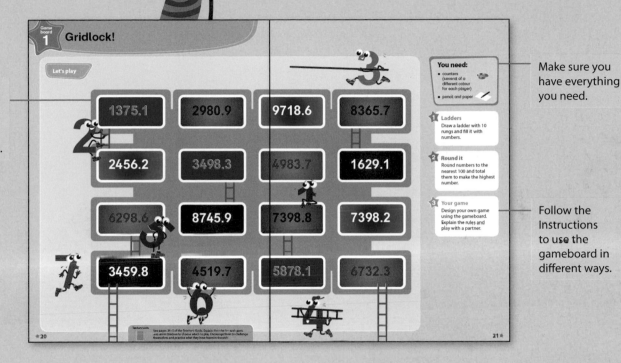

Make sure you have everything you need.

Follow the Instructions to use the gameboard in different ways.

Try these activities to check what you have learnt in the unit. Have you understood all the new maths concepts?

Find out more about maths by reading these fun facts!

# Problem solving and reasoning

Try these ideas to develop your reasoning skills. Doing this will help you improve your mathematical thinking.

**Make statements**
Can you say what you notice about why something happens?

**Convince**
Can you persuade other people that your statements are correct?

**Organise**
Can you put things into groups, an order or a pattern?

**Generalise**
Can you make connections to describe rules and patterns?

**Classify**
Can you identify and name the groups you have organised things into?

**Find examples**
Can you give specific examples to fit a pattern or rule?

**Imagine**
Can you think of different ideas or ways to do things?

**Explain**
Can you explain your thinking and reasoning about a problem?

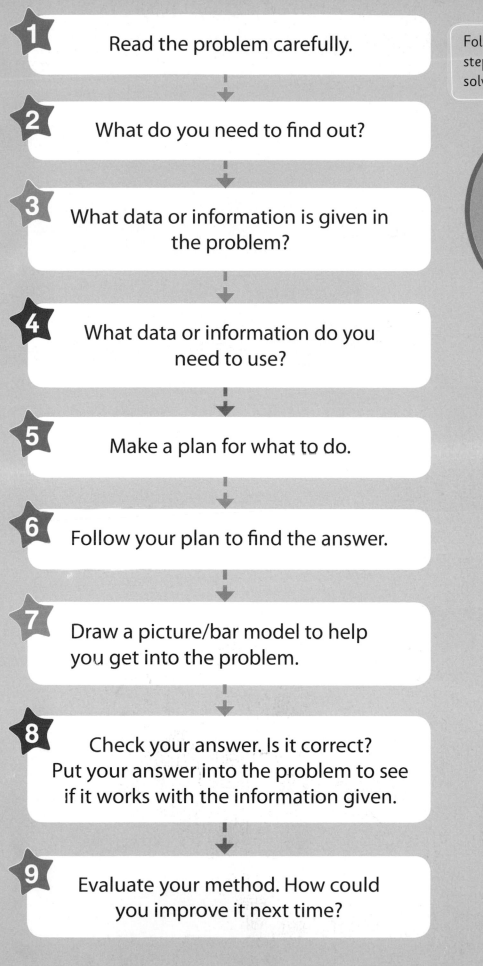

1 Read the problem carefully.

2 What do you need to find out?

3 What data or information is given in the problem?

4 What data or information do you need to use?

5 Make a plan for what to do.

6 Follow your plan to find the answer.

7 Draw a picture/bar model to help you get into the problem.

8 Check your answer. Is it correct? Put your answer into the problem to see if it works with the information given.

9 Evaluate your method. How could you improve it next time?

Follow these steps to help you solve problems!

# Numbers in real life

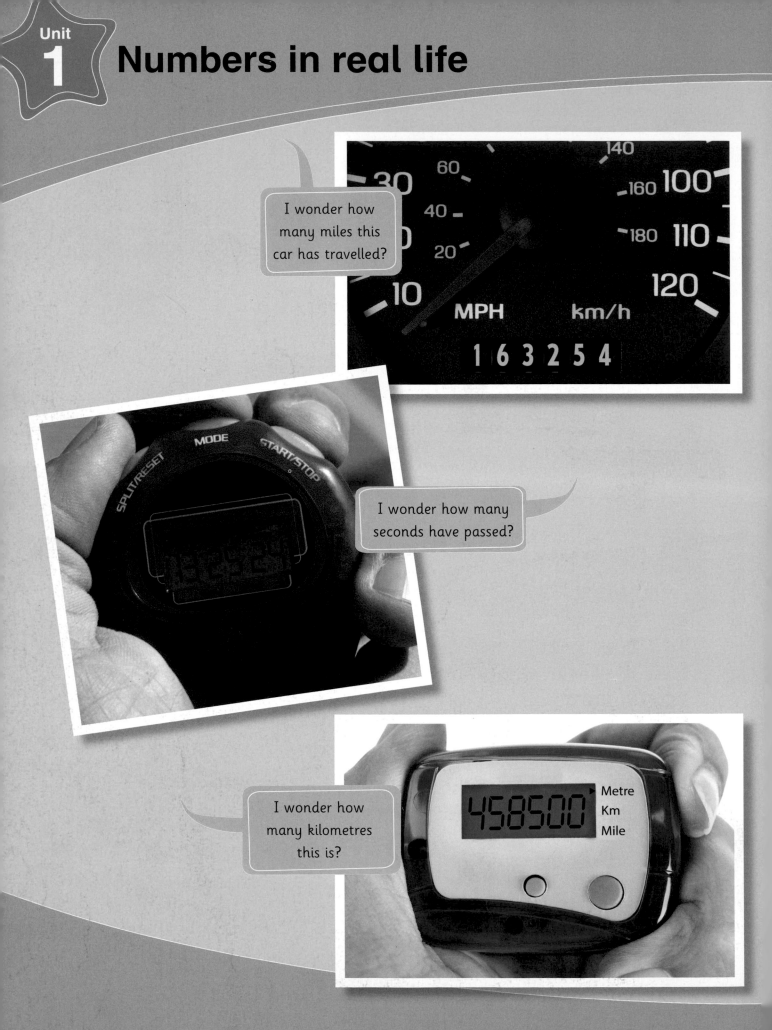

How can you find the distance from Exeter to St. Ives?

I wonder what these prices would be rounded to the nearest pound?

Teacher's Guide
Look at the pictures with the children and discuss the questions.
See pages 24–5 of the *Teacher's Guide* for key ideas to draw out.

11

**Let's learn**

**You need:**
- digit cards
- place-value grid
- ruler

I'd say it's about 9000 km from London to Cape Town.

I don't think that's right. You need to round to the nearest thousand kilometres. 635 is closer to 1000 than zero, so 9635 is closer to 10000 than 9000.

| To/from | Canberra | New Delhi | Paris | Cape Town | Athens | London |
|---|---|---|---|---|---|---|
| London | 16976 km | 6724 km | 343 km | 9635 km | 2394 km | |
| New Delhi | 10338 km | | 6601 km | 9286 km | 5020 km | 6724 km |

## Ordering and comparing

To order and compare numbers you need to look at the place value.

Compare the 2 distances to Cape Town.

The thousands numbers are the same, so you need to look at the hundreds.

| | | 1000 | 100 | 10 | 1 |
|---|---|---|---|---|---|
| London | | 9 | ⑥ | 3 | 5 |
| New Delhi | | 9 | ② | 8 | 6 |

London to Cape Town has 6 and New Delhi to Cape Town has 2 in the hundreds column. The first distance is the greatest.

You can write comparisons like this: 9635 > 9286 or 9286 < 9635.

## Rounding

0  10  20  30  40  50  60  70  80  90  100

34 is closer to 30 than 40 so round down to 30.

68 is closer to 70 than 60 so round up to 70.

55 is in the middle so round up to 60.

What would these numbers round to?

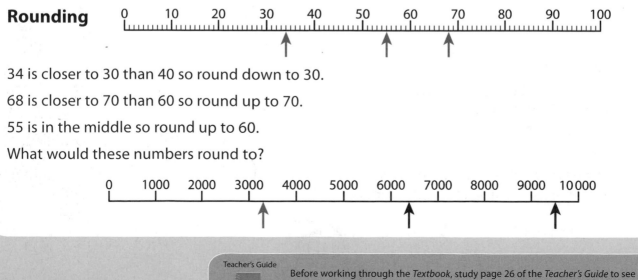

0  1000  2000  3000  4000  5000  6000  7000  8000  9000  10000

Teacher's Guide

Before working through the *Textbook*, study page 26 of the *Teacher's Guide* to see how the concepts should be introduced. Read and discuss the page with the children. Provide concrete resources to support exploration.

**1**

### Order.

Order these numbers from smallest to greatest.

a   2465, 2152, 2985, 2456, 2125, 2859

b   12356, 12391, 12501, 12365, 12319, 12510

c   124132, 142132, 124123, 142123, 124312, 142312

Order the same numbers again, rounding them to the nearest 100 first.

What do you notice?

Remember to compare the place value carefully!

**2**

### Round and order.

a   Round all the distances in the table on the opposite page to the nearest 10 kilometres.

b   Order them from greatest to smallest or smallest to greatest.

**3**

### Measure.

Draw 10 curvy lines something like this:

Use a piece of string and a ruler to measure their lengths. Write down the lengths and then round them to make an approximation.

**4**

### Investigate.

London is 9635 km from Cape Town.
Find distances from 1 country to another which are greater than this.

Use the Internet or holiday brochures to find out the distances between different places!

List these distances. Then, compare them using the greater than and less than symbols.

Teacher's Guide

See page 27 of the *Teacher's Guide* for ideas of how to guide practice. Work through each step together as a class to develop children's conceptual understanding.

13

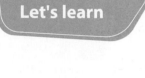
**Let's learn**

I converted 1.5 km into metres and centimetres and I got 1500 m and 15 000 cm.

I don't think that's right. There are 100 centimetres in a metre, so you need to multiply the metre amount by 100.

**You need:**
- place-value grid
- geared clock

## Converting between kilometres, metres and centimetres

### 1 km = 1000 m

To convert from kilometres to metres you multiply the kilometres by 1000.

1.5 km multiplied by 1000 (or 10 and 10 and 10 again) is 1500 m.

### 1 m = 100 cm

| 1000 | 100 | 10 | 1 | . | $\frac{1}{10}$ |
|------|-----|----|----|----|----|
|      |     |    | 1 | . | 5 |
| 1    | 5   | 0  | 0 |   |   |

To convert from metres to centimetres multiply by 100.

1500 m multiplied by by 100 (or 10 and 10) is 150 000 cm.

1.5 km = 1500 m = 150 000 cm

Use a place-value grid to convert 2.75 km and 2750 m to centimetres.

| 100 000 | 10 000 | 1000 | 100 | 10 | 1 |
|---------|--------|------|-----|----|----|
|         |        | 1    | 5   | 0  | 0 |
| 1       | 5      | 0    | 0   | 0  | 0 |

## Converting between units of time

### 1 minute = 60 seconds        1 hour = 60 minutes

Converting units of time is different to converting other units of measure. To convert between hours, minutes and seconds you work in Base 60, and multiply by 60 to convert to a smaller unit.

To convert 5 minutes to seconds, multiply 5 by 60.

5 minutes = 300 seconds

How many seconds are there in 8 hours?

Teacher's Guide
Before working through the *Textbook*, study page 28 of the *Teacher's Guide* to see how the concepts should be introduced. Read and discuss the page with the children. Provide concrete resources to support exploration.

**1**

## Convert.

**a**   Kilometres to metres:
3.5 km
4.25 km
12 km
15.1 km
25.125 km

**b**   Metres to centimetres:
24 m, 12.6 m, 18.3 m, 5.05 m, 15.23 m

**c**   Kilometres to centimetres:
1 km, 2.3 km, 5.4 km, 10.1 km, 11.05 km

**2**

## Convert.

**a**   Minutes to seconds:
3 minutes, 12 minutes, 25 minutes, $8\frac{1}{2}$ minutes, $15\frac{1}{2}$ minutes

**b**   Hours to minutes:
8 hours, 14 hours, 16 hours 15 minutes, 20 hours 45 minutes, 24 hours

**3**

## Apply.

4 friends compared how long their homework took. Freddy thought he had spent the longest on it. Is he right?

Use a stop watch to time yourself and your partner as you carry out an activity of your choice. Write down the time in minutes and seconds and then convert it to seconds.

| Name | Time taken |
|------|-----------|
| Freddy | 72 minutes |
| Bianca | $1\frac{1}{2}$ hour |
| Opal | 4500 seconds |
| Ben | 1 hour 10 minutes |

**4**

## Investigate.

On a 24-hour clock, at certain times, all the digits are consecutive.

Can you find all of them? You can count forwards or backwards.

Here are 2 examples, 4:56 and 5:43.

Teacher's Guide

See page 29 of the *Teacher's Guide* for ideas of how to guide practice.
Work through each step together as a class to develop children's
conceptual understanding.

# Fraction and decimal equivalences

**Let's learn**

**You need:**
- place-value grids
- digit cards
- place-value charts
- weighing scales

A packet of rice says 1.5 kg. That's the same as 1 and $\frac{5}{100}$ isn't it?

I don't think so. 0.5 is the same as $\frac{1}{2}$ which is equivalent to $\frac{5}{10}$ and $\frac{50}{100}$. So, 1.5 must be equivalent to 1 and $\frac{5}{10}$.

## Writing decimal numbers as fractions

| 10 | 1 | . | $\frac{1}{10}$ | $\frac{1}{100}$ |
|---|---|---|---|---|
| 2 | 4 | . | 3 | |
| 1 | 5 | . | 2 | 5 |

Numbers to the right of ones are tenths, then hundredths, then thousandths, and so on.

The place-value grid helps show equivalences between decimals and fractions.

The decimal point separates whole numbers from part numbers (decimal fractions).

$24.3 = 24$ and $\frac{3}{10}$

$15.25 = 15$ and $\frac{25}{100}$

## Comparing thousandths with hundredths and tenths

| | | | | | | | | |
|---|---|---|---|---|---|---|---|---|
| 0.01 | 0.02 | 0.03 | 0.04 | 0.05 | 0.06 | 0.07 | 0.08 | 0.09 |
| 0.1 | 0.2 | 0.3 | 0.4 | 0.5 | 0.6 | 0.7 | 0.8 | 0.9 |
| 1 | 2 | 3 | 4 | 5 | 6 | 7 | 8 | 9 |
| 10 | 20 | 30 | 40 | 50 | 60 | 70 | 80 | 90 |
| 100 | 200 | 300 | 400 | 500 | 600 | 700 | 800 | 900 |

10 tenths make 1 whole. 10 hundredths make 1 tenth and 100 hundredths make 1 whole.

Can you see a pattern? How many thousandths make 1 whole?

How many thousandths make $\frac{1}{100}$?

What about $\frac{1}{10}$?

Teacher's Guide

Before working through the *Textbook*, study page 30 of the *Teacher's Guide* to see how the concepts should be introduced. Read and discuss the page with the children. Provide concrete resources to support exploration.

**1**

**Write.**

Write these decimals as fractions.

a   1.2          d   15.4          g   3.45          j   18.37

b   3.5          e   25.8          h   12.62

c   14.6         f   2.25          i   16.28

**2**

**Write.**

Write these thousandths as hundredths. Explain how you did this.

a   $\frac{240}{1000}$          c   $\frac{620}{1000}$          e   $\frac{870}{1000}$

b   $\frac{410}{1000}$          d   $\frac{350}{1000}$

Write these thousandths as tenths.  Explain how you did this.

f   $\frac{200}{1000}$          h   $\frac{600}{1000}$          j   $\frac{900}{1000}$

g   $\frac{400}{1000}$          i   $\frac{700}{1000}$

**3**

**Measure.**

Collect 5 items from around your classroom and find the mass of each item in grams.

Convert the masses from grams to kilograms.

Record the masses with decimal fractions.

1 kilogram = 1000 grams.
Use a place-value grid to
help you!

**4**

**Think.**

Use these digits to make up all the masses you can that have 2 decimal places.

Once you have written your masses, order them from lowest to highest mass.

Teacher's Guide
See page 31 of the *Teacher's Guide* for ideas of how to guide practice.
Work through each step together as a class to develop children's
conceptual understanding.

17 ★

# Reading, writing and ordering decimal numbers

**Let's learn**

**You need:**
- digit cards
- 4 differently-sized containers or bottles
- measuring jug

I think 1986.5 is smaller than 1986.45 because 45 is larger than 5.

I don't agree! The 5 in your number is 5 tenths and the 4 is 4 tenths. So I think that 1986.5 is the larger number.

## Comparing and ordering decimal numbers

Comparing and ordering decimal numbers is similar to comparing and ordering whole numbers.

Look at each digit in turn from the highest to the lowest. When you find 2 digits that are different, the highest means that this number is higher than the other one.

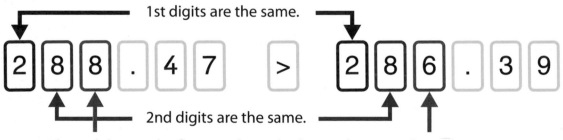

1st digits are the same.

$$2\ 8\ 8\ .\ 4\ 7\quad>\quad 2\ 8\ 6\ .\ 3\ 9$$

2nd digits are the same.

The 3rd digit in the first number is higher in the second number.

## Rounding decimal numbers

Rounding decimal numbers is similar to rounding whole numbers.

To round a number with 1 decimal place, look at the tenths. If it is less than 5, round down. If it is 5 or higher, round up. In this example, round 145.6 up to 146 km. Round 145.3 km down to 145 km.

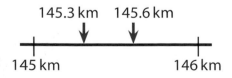

145.3 km    145.6 km

145 km            146 km

To round a number with 2 decimal places, do the same thing but with the hundredths, e.g. 145.56 round up to 145.6, 896.73 round down to 896.7.

Teacher's Guide

Before working through the *Textbook*, study page 32 of the *Teacher's Guide* to see how the concepts should be introduced. Read and discuss the page with the children. Provide concrete resources to support exploration.

**1**

## Complete.

Use the >, < and = symbols to complete these number statements.

a    25.5 + 25.4 ☐ 25.5 + 25.4        d    15.25 + 12.32 ☐ 15.25 + 12.98

b    30.6 + 21.3 ☐ 30.6 + 23.7        e    30.16 + 14.32 ☐ 30.14 + 14.34

c    14.4 + 14.5 ☐ 14.2 + 14.7

**2**

## Round.

Round these numbers to the nearest whole number.

a    35.8          c    279.9          e    3678.4

b    49.2          d    478.5

> Remember to round down if it's less than 5 and to round up if it's 5 or higher!

Round these numbers to the nearest tenth.

f    145.23        h    546.77         j    5678.85

g    459.39        i    1526.23

**3**

## Measure.

Choose 4 bottles or containers and pour water into each one.

Use a measuring jug to measure the volume of water in each container and round it up or down to the nearest litre.

**4**

## Think.

Freddy lost the labels showing the amounts of liquids in 4 bottles. He knew that the largest measurement was 900 ml and that the smallest was 150 ml. All the measurements were in multiples of 75 ml. What could the other measurements have been?

Teacher's Guide
See page 33 of the *Teacher's Guide* for ideas of how to guide practice. Work through each step together as a class to develop children's conceptual understanding.

19 ★

# Gridlock!

Let's play

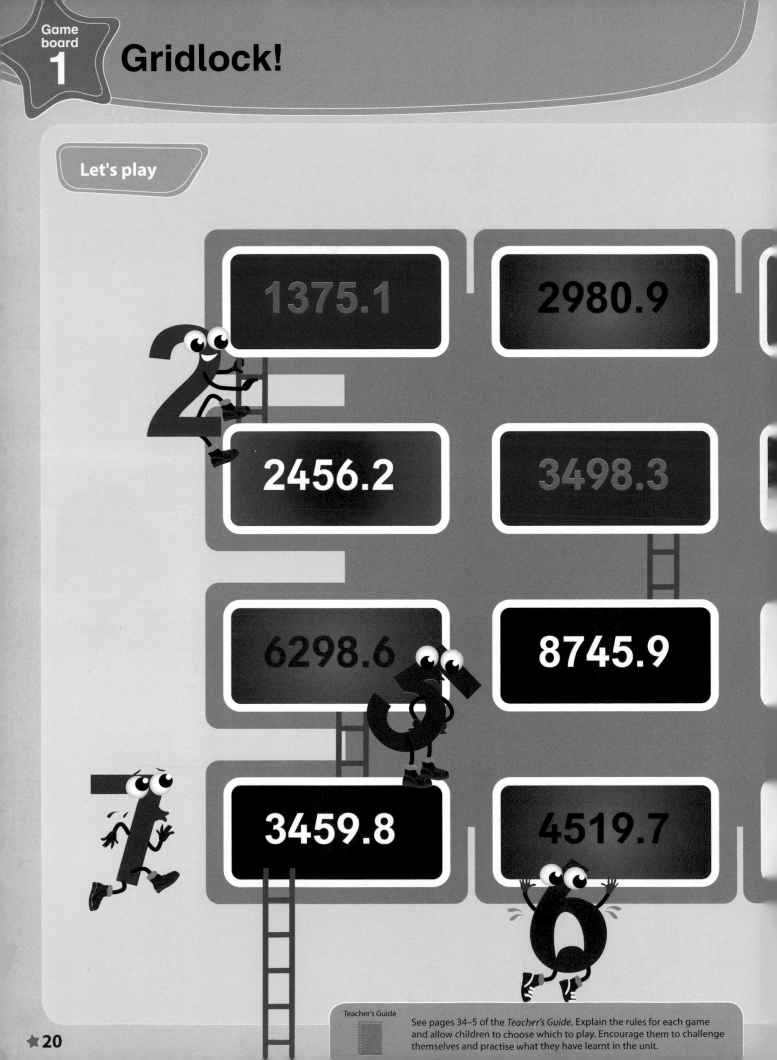

1375.1

2980.9

2456.2

3498.3

6298.6

8745.9

3459.8

4519.7

Teacher's Guide

See pages 34–5 of the *Teacher's Guide*. Explain the rules for each game and allow children to choose which to play. Encourage them to challenge themselves and practise what they have learnt in the unit.

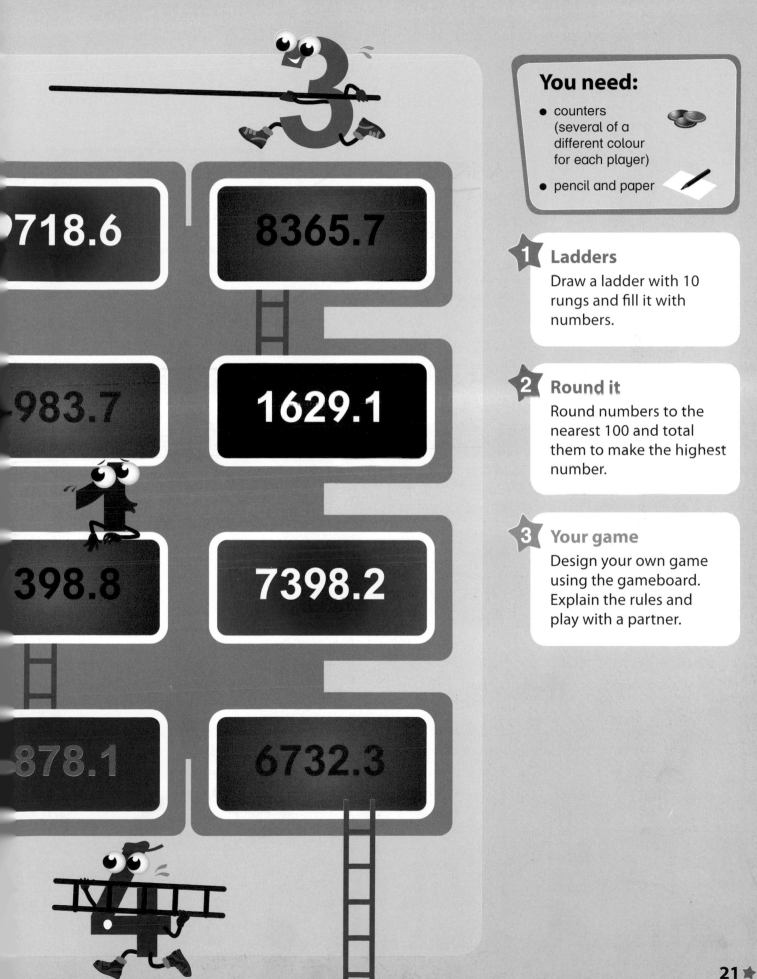

9718.6

8365.7

983.7

1629.1

398.8

7398.2

878.1

6732.3

**1 Ladders**

Draw a ladder with 10 rungs and fill it with numbers.

**2 Round it**

Round numbers to the nearest 100 and total them to make the highest number.

**3 Your game**

Design your own game using the gameboard. Explain the rules and play with a partner.

# And finally ...

Let's review

**1**

245 679 rounded to the nearest thousand is 245 000.

Explain why Amy is wrong and what the correct answer should be.

**You need:**
- digit cards
- place-value grids

**2**

| 13.5 | 15.1 | 21.9 | 8.4 | 22.7 | 7.6 |

< > = + −

**You need:**
- digit cards
- place-value cards

Use the symbols to compare these numbers.
Make 2 statements for each number.

Now use digit cards to make up 5 of your own numbers with 2 decimal places. Make up some comparison statements with them.

Teacher's Guide

See pages 36–7 of the *Teacher's Guide* for guidance on running each task.
Observe children to identify those who have mastered concepts and those who require further consolidation.

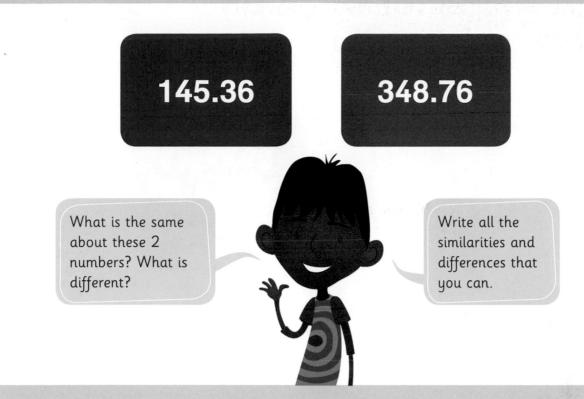

**145.36**

**348.76**

What is the same about these 2 numbers? What is different?

Write all the similarities and differences that you can.

# Did you know?

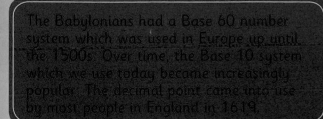

The Babylonians had a Base 60 number system which was used in Europe up until the 1500s. Over time, the Base 10 system which we use today became increasingly popular. The decimal point came into use by most people in England in 1619.

What do you think the Base 60 numbers 60 and 360 are in our number system?

# Methods for addition and subtraction

Could you work out how much it will cost to buy one of each roll of wallpaper?

£15.99
25 m

£11.99
40 m

£12.99
30 m

£14.99
15 m

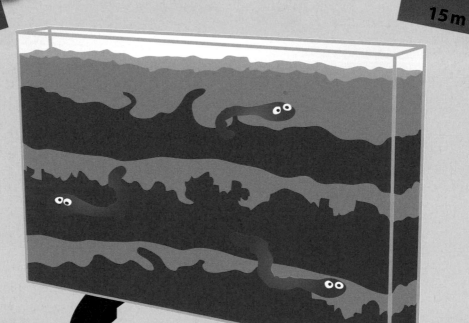

I wonder what the difference in length is between the longest and the shortest worm?

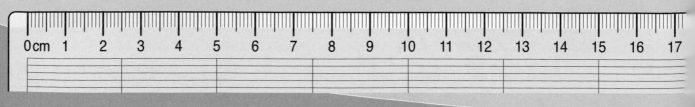

0 cm 1 2 3 4 5 6 7 8 9 10 11 12 13 14 15 16 17

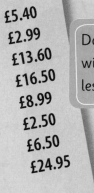

**Jo's Pizza Place**

| | |
|---|---|
| 2 garlic bread | £5.40 |
| 1 olives | £2.99 |
| 2 pizza margherita | £13.60 |
| 2 pizza calzone | £16.50 |
| 1 spaghetti | £8.99 |
| 1 side salad | £2.50 |
| 2 ice cream | £6.50 |
| 5 fruit cocktails | £24.95 |

Do you think the bill will come to more or less than £100?

regular unleaded 115.6

regular diesel 113.8

I wonder how much more it will cost to buy a litre of diesel than a litre of unleaded petrol?

Teacher's Guide

Look at the pictures with the children and discuss the questions.
See pages 38–9 of the *Teacher's Guide* for key ideas to draw out.

# Written methods for addition and subtraction

**Let's learn**

**You need:**
- sets of digit cards
- place-value grids
- Base 10 apparatus
- place-value counters
- dice

I think if I add 210.9 and 423.8, I will get 633.17. Am I right?

```
  210.9
+ 423.8
  633.17
```

```
  210.9
+ 423.8
  634.7
    1
```

Almost, but you have forgotten to carry the tenths over into the next column. The answer is actually 634.7.

## Written method for addition

To add using the written method you must add the least significant digits first. If you add 9 tenths and 8 tenths you get 17 tenths. You exchange 10 tenths for one.

```
  256.9
+ 167.8
      7
    1
```

Next you add the ones which total 14. You exchange 10 ones for a ten and put that in the tens position.

```
  256.9
+ 167.8
    4.7
   1 1
```

Then you add the tens which totals 12. You exchange 10 tens for one hundred. Then you add the hundreds which is 4.

```
  256.9
+ 167.8
  424.7
  1 1 1
```

Make up some decimal numbers to add together like this.

## Written method for subtraction

You can also use a written method to find the difference between two numbers.

Start in the tenths column. If you can't subtract the lower number from the higher number you must exchange one for 10 tenths. Do the same if you need to in the ones, tens and hundreds columns.

```
  4 3⁴5̷.¹8
- 1 3 7.9
  3 0 7.9
```

Make up some decimal subtraction calculations to answer.

Teacher's Guide

Before working through the *Textbook*, study page 42 of the *Teacher's Guide* to see how the concepts should be introduced. Read and discuss the page with the children. Provide concrete resources to support exploration.

**1**

## Calculate.

Add these numbers using
the written method.

a    8587 + 7487

b    10 645 + 9374

c    23 465 + 21 937

d    46 395 + 35 487

Subtract these numbers using
the written method.

e    7350 – 3754

f    8751 – 4846

g    19 475 – 9586

h    54 735 – 37 738

**2**

## Answer these.

a    Holly saved up £156.
She spent £98.75 on a DVD player. How
much money did she have left?

b    Arjan had £465. He spent £296.50 on a
push bike. How much did he have left?

c    Ben spent £568 on a TV.
He had £234.67 left. How much money
did he start off with?

d    Kitty saved £156.45. She wanted to buy
a laptop. The laptop costs £250. How
much more money does she need?

**3**

## Solve.

Find the missing digits in these
calculations.

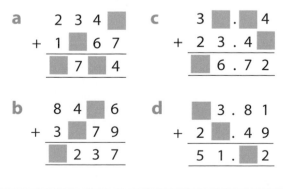

**4**

## Think.

Draw a grid like this on paper.

| | | |
|---|---|---|
| | | |

Throw a dice 6 times. Put 1 digit in each
square of the grid to make an addition
calculation. Your aim is to get as close to
1000 as you can. Add the 2 numbers. Try this
5 times to see how successful you can be.

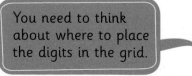

You need to think
about where to place
the digits in the grid.

Teacher's Guide

See page 43 of the *Teacher's Guide* for ideas of how to guide practice.
Work through each step together as a class to develop children's
conceptual understanding.

29 ★

# Follow the instructions!

Let's play

Start  −123  +199  double it  +298

−222  double it  +799  −496  −201

−321

double it

+444  +123  −396  double it  −398

Teacher's Guide

See pages 44–5 of the *Teacher's Guide*. Explain the rules for each game and allow children to choose which to play. Encourage them to challenge themselves and practise what they have learnt in the unit.

+333  −199  −111

double it

+397

double it  +403  −299

399  double it  **Finish**

**1  Highest wins**

Place your counters on Start. Use the digit cards to make a 4-digit number and move around the board. The player with the highest number at the end wins!

**2  Lowest wins**

Each player starts with 1000 points. The player with the lowest number at the end wins!

**3  Your game**

Design your own game. Explain the rules and play with a partner.

**Let's review**

**1**

In this unit you have looked at lots of mental calculation strategies for addition and subtraction. You have explored:

- adding and subtracting a near multiple of ten and adjusting
- sequencing
- counting on
- near doubling.

Now is the time to show what you have remembered!

I can subtract 4999 from 5876 using a mental calculation strategy.

Explain why Amy is correct and the mental calculation strategy she could use.

Can you think of another strategy she could use? Explain what this could be.

**2**

Write down an example of 2 numbers that can be added using the near double strategy.

Now write down another...

And another...

And another...

And another!

Make sure all your examples have different numbers of digits.

Teacher's Guide

See pages 46–7 of the *Teacher's Guide* for guidance on running each task. Observe children to identify those who have mastered concepts and those who require further consolidation.

**3**

Show how you can answer this calculation in 4 different ways:

**2387 + 1996**

Which do you think is the most efficient method? Why?

Show how you can answer this calculation in 4 different ways:

**5245 – 4999**

Which do you think is the most efficient method? Why?

Show how you can answer this calculation in 4 different ways:

**2500 + 2600**

Which do you think is the most efficient method? Why?

Show how you can answer this calculation in 4 different ways:

**7000 – 3500**

Which do you think is the most efficient method? Why?

# Did you know?

Formal written methods for adding and subtracting have been around for years. These are called algorithms. An algorithm is a list of rules to follow with steps in the right order. They apply to most things we do every day, even brushing your teeth!

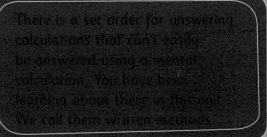

There is a set order for answering calculations that can't easily be answered using a mental calculation. You have been learning about these in this unit. We call them written methods.

# Methods for multiplication and division

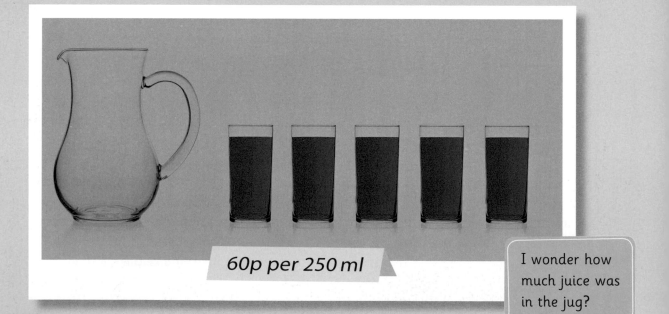

How can I find out how many cups there are without counting every one?

60p per 250 ml

I wonder how much juice was in the jug?

My flapjack recipe needs 250 g of oats. How many batches could I make?

1.5 kg

Apparently, this pizza has an area of 144 cm². I wonder how I could prove that it was true?

Teacher's Guide
Look at the pictures with the children and discuss the questions.
See pages 48–9 of the *Teacher's Guide* for key ideas to draw out.

35

**Let's learn**

**You need:**
- sets of digit cards
- rulers
- interlocking cubes
- squared paper

I think that 5 squared is 10 and 5 cubed is 15.

That's not quite right. 'Squared' means that you multiply the number by itself. 'Cubed' means you multiply the number by itself twice.

## Square and cube numbers

A square number is the product of a number that has been multiplied by itself. Square numbers can be arranged into a square array:

1
$1 \times 1 = 1$

4
$2 \times 2 = 4$

9
$3 \times 3 = 9$

16
$4 \times 4 = 16$

A cube number is the product of a number multiplied by itself twice, e.g. $3 \times 3 \times 3 = 27$

This is a diagram of a cube number:

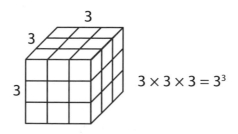

$3 \times 3 \times 3 = 3^3$

## Multiples and factors

A multiple is a number divisible by another with no remainder.

A factor is a number that will divide exactly into another number.

24 is a multiple of 1, 2, 3, 4, 6, 8, 12 and 24.

These numbers are also factors of 24!

Write down all the factors of 32.

Teacher's Guide

Before working through the *Textbook*, study page 50 of the *Teacher's Guide* to see how the concepts should be introduced. Read and discuss the page with the children. Provide concrete resources to support exploration.

## 1

### Answer these.

a Which are square numbers?
15, 36, 81, 24, 56, 100

b Which are cube numbers?
1, 24, 27, 60, 125, 1000

c Write down the first 10 multiples of 6 and 8.

d Now circle the common multiples.

## 2

### Answer these.

Write down 5 multiples of:

a 4          c 6          e 7

b 8          d 5          f 9

Write down all the factors of:

g 36          i 12          k 44

h 28          j 72          l 54

## 3

### Apply.

Draw 6 squares that have sides of these lengths:

a 4 cm

b 8 cm

c 12 cm

d 15 cm

e 20 cm

f 25 cm

Now work out their areas.

## 4

### Think.

Choose 6 square numbers.
Write down their factors. What do you notice?
Write a statement to show this.

Choose 6 numbers that aren't square numbers.
Write down their factors. What do you notice?
Write a statement to show this.

Teacher's Guide
See page 51 of the *Teacher's Guide* for ideas of how to guide practice.
Work through each step together as a class to develop children's conceptual understanding.

37

**Let's learn**

I want to multiply 243 by 5. That's a big number so I'll need to use a written method!

No you don't! You should look at a calculation and decide on the best method to use. Here, 5 is half of 10, so you could multiply 243 by 10 and halve it, or halve it and multiply by 10.

## Multiplying by 5 and 20

Half of 10 is 5. To multiply by 5, multiply the number by 10 and halve it, or halve the number first and then multiply it by 10.

Make up some numbers and multiply them by 5 using this strategy.

To divide by 5, you do the opposite: divide by 10 and double.

20 is double 10. To multiply by 20, multiply by 10 and double, or double and then multiply by 10.

Make some numbers and multiply them by 20 using this strategy.

To divide by 20, you do the opposite: divide by 10 and halve it.

## Using known facts

Multiplication or division facts can be used to generate other facts.

Whatever you do to one side of the equals sign, you must do to the other.

Make up some more facts in a similar way. This will keep the equivalence.

| $8 \times 9 = 72$ | Double 8 and the answer to give $16 \times 9 = 144$ | Halve 9 and 144 to give $16 \times 4.5 = 72$ | Multiply 4.5 by 10 to give $16 \times 45 = 720$ |

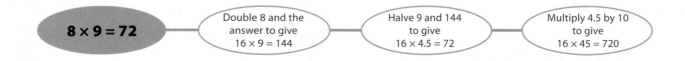

Teacher's Guide

Before working through the *Textbook*, study page 52 of the *Teacher's Guide* to see how the concepts should be introduced. Read and discuss the page with the children. Provide concrete resources to support exploration.

## 1

### Multiply.

Multiply these numbers by 5.
Use the multiplying by 10 and halving strategy.

a    48

b    286

c    864

d    4140

Multiply these numbers by 20.
Use the multiplying by 10 and doubling strategy:

e    54

f    136

g    487

h    2874

## 2

### Divide.

Divide these numbers by 5.
Use the dividing by 10 and doubling strategy:

a    40

b    180

c    380

d    4620

Divide these numbers by 20.
Use the dividing by 10 and halving strategy:

e    40

f    200

g    840

h    2420

## 3

### Draw.

6 cm × 7          3 cm × 12

5 cm × 8          4 cm × 9

Draw the products as lines in order from shortest to longest.

56 cm ÷ 7

72 cm ÷ 6

121 cm ÷ 12

Draw the products as lines in order from longest to shortest.

## 4

### Think.

I thought of a multiplication fact. I multiplied one number by 10, halved the other and then doubled both numbers. This is the number statement I was left with: $120 \times 9 = 540$.

What was the original multiplication fact?

Could Theo have started with a different multiplication fact?

Teacher's Guide
See page 53 of the *Teacher's Guide* for ideas of how to guide practice. Work through each step together as a class to develop children's conceptual understanding.

39

# Written methods for multiplication and division

**Let's learn**

I worked out the answer to this calculation!

$$456 \\ \times \ 6 \over 2436$$

**You need:**
- digit cards `1` `3` `5`
- counters (3 colours)

That's not quite right. 400 × 6 is 2400 and 50 × 6 is 300. You need to add the 300 to 2400 so the answer will be 2 thousand 7 hundred and something. I don't think you have exchanged where you needed to.

## Multiplication

This array shows 145 × 3. There are 3 hundreds, 12 tens and 15 ones.

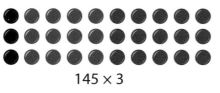

145 × 3

You can add the numbers together to make a number statement:
300 + 120 + 15 = 435.

This can be shown using the grid method:

|      | 100 | 40  | 5  |
|------|-----|-----|----|
| × 3  | 300 | 120 | 15 |

You can also use a written column method:

$$\begin{array}{r} 1\,4\,5 \\ \times \quad 3 \\ \hline 4\,3\,5 \\ {\scriptstyle 1\ 1} \end{array}$$

What is the same and what is different about these 3 ways of multiplying?

## Division

The division calculation 192 ÷ 6 can be shown using counters and the short written method.

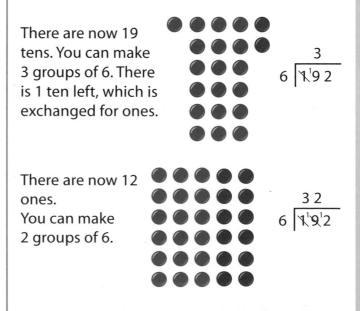

$6\,\overline{)\,1\,9\,2}$

You can't make 6 groups of 100 so need to change the one hundred into tens.

There are now 19 tens. You can make 3 groups of 6. There is 1 ten left, which is exchanged for ones.

$6\,\overline{)\,\cancel{1}^{\,1}9\,2}$ $\quad^{3}$

There are now 12 ones. You can make 2 groups of 6.

$6\,\overline{)\,\cancel{1}^{\,1}9\,2}$ $\quad^{3\,2}$

**Teacher's Guide**
Before working through the *Textbook*, study page 54 of the *Teacher's Guide* to see how the concepts should be introduced. Read and discuss the page with the children. Provide concrete resources to support exploration.

★ **40**

**1**

**Calculate.** Answer these calculations using counters.
Record the answer using the grid method. Check your answer using the column method.

a    64 × 6        c    326 × 4        e    635 × 8

b    135 × 3       d    427 × 7        f    429 × 9

**2**

**Calculate.** Answer these calculations using counters.
Record what you did using the short written method.

a    96 ÷ 4        c    184 ÷ 4        e    847 ÷ 7

b    132 ÷ 3       d    672 ÷ 6        f    976 ÷ 8

**3**

**Investigate.**

Work out the products of these measurements:

a    345 m × 6

b    256 g × 4

c    259 ml × 5

Now work out the quotients of these.
Write any remainders beside the quotient.

d    145 m ÷ 7

e    978 g ÷ 8

f    918 g ÷ 9

Now draw 5 lines that are between 100 mm and 300 mm in length. Multiply each by 9. What are the new measurements?
Now divide each by 10. Draw these lines. What is the difference between your 2 measurements?

**4**

**Think.**
Find the missing digits.

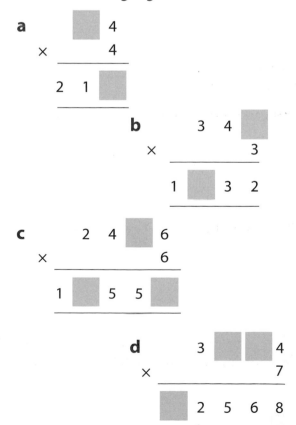

Teacher's Guide    See page 55 of the *Teacher's Guide* for ideas of how to guide practice.
Work through each step together as a class to develop children's conceptual understanding.

**41** ★

# Head for the stars!

**1** Pick 4
Make a 3-digit number. Multiply it by the 4th card.

**2** Pick 3
Make a 2-digit number. Divide it by the 3rd card.

**4** Pick 4
Make a 3-digit number. Multiply it by the 4th card.

**5** Pick 1
Cube the number.

**6** Pick 1
Cube the number.

**9** Pick 2
Make a 2-digit number. Write down its factors.

**10** Pick 3
Make a 2-digit number. Divide it by the 3rd card.

**13** Pick 4
Make square numbers.

**14** Pick 3
Make a 2-digit number. Divide it by the 3rd card.

Teacher's Guide See pages 56–7 of the *Teacher's Guide*. Explain the rules for each game and allow children to choose which to play. Encourage them to challenge themselves and practise what they have learnt in the unit.

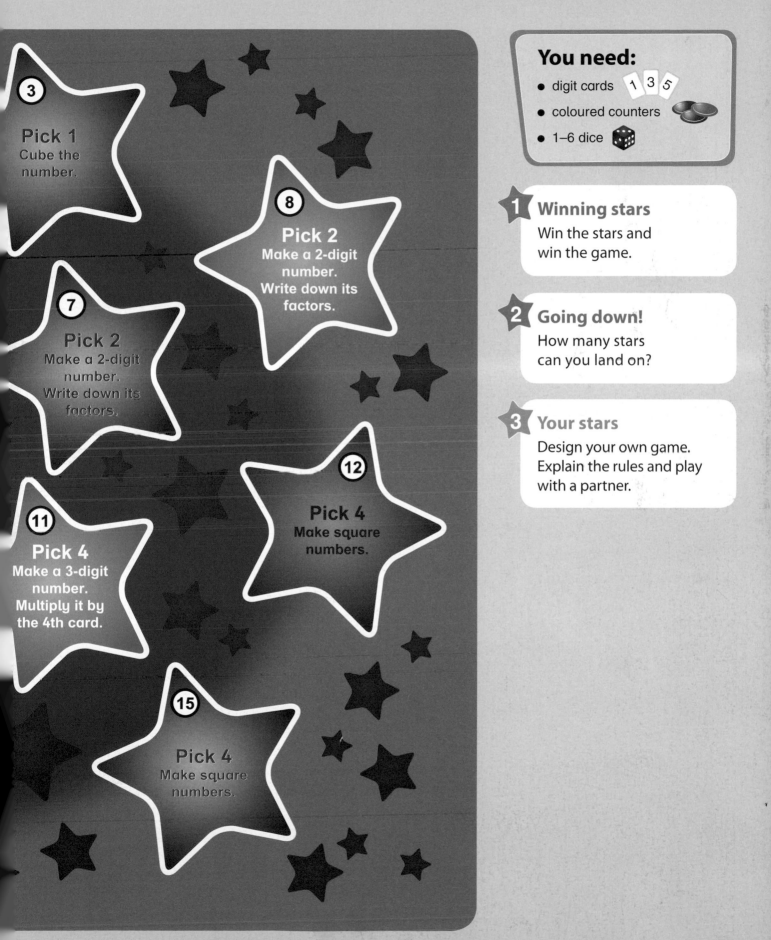

**3** Pick 1
Cube the number.

**8** Pick 2
Make a 2-digit number.
Write down its factors.

**7** Pick 2
Make a 2-digit number.
Write down its factors.

**11** Pick 4
Make a 3-digit number.
Multiply it by the 4th card.

**12** Pick 4
Make square numbers.

**15** Pick 4
Make square numbers.

**You need:**
- digit cards  1 3 5
- coloured counters
- 1–6 dice

**1** **Winning stars**
Win the stars and win the game.

**2** **Going down!**
How many stars can you land on?

**3** **Your stars**
Design your own game.
Explain the rules and play with a partner.

# And finally …

**1**

I think 4, 6 and 10 are factors of 60.

Is Theo correct?

Explain why.

Write down all the other factors of 60.

**2**

Write down an example of a fact that you can make using $8 \times 5 = 40$.

Now write down another…

And another…

And another…

Make sure all your examples are made in different ways.

Write down an example of a fact that you can make using $54 \div 9 = 6$.

Now write down another…

And another…

And another…

Make sure all your examples are made in different ways.

Don't forget, you can multiply, double and halve!

Teacher's Guide

See pages 58–9 of the *Teacher's Guide* for guidance on running each task. Observe children to identify those who have mastered concepts and those who require further consolidation.

**3**

Show how you can answer these calculations in 4 different ways:

468 × 4

675 ÷ 5

For each one, which do you think is the most efficient way? Why is that?

# Did you know?

In the past, different civilisations had other ways of multiplying and dividing numbers. The Ancient Egyptians would multiply and divide by doubling.

I want to multiply 6 by 36.

They would begin with 36 and double it. They would double it again and again, each time writing the number of 36s that had been doubled and then choose those numbers that added up to 6 and add their multiples.

2 + 4 = **6**
72 + 144 = **216**
so 6 × 36 = 216

1    36
2    72
4    144
8    288

# Triangles – and other polygons

I wonder if there are other buildings that are regular polygons?

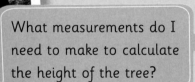

What measurements do I need to make to calculate the height of the tree?

I wonder what polygons I can find in the pylon structure?

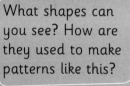

What shapes can you see? How are they used to make patterns like this?

Are the patterns on giraffes polygons? Where else do you find polygons in the natural world?

Teacher's Guide
Look at the pictures with the children and discuss the questions.
See pages 60–1 of the *Teacher's Guide* for key ideas to draw out.

47

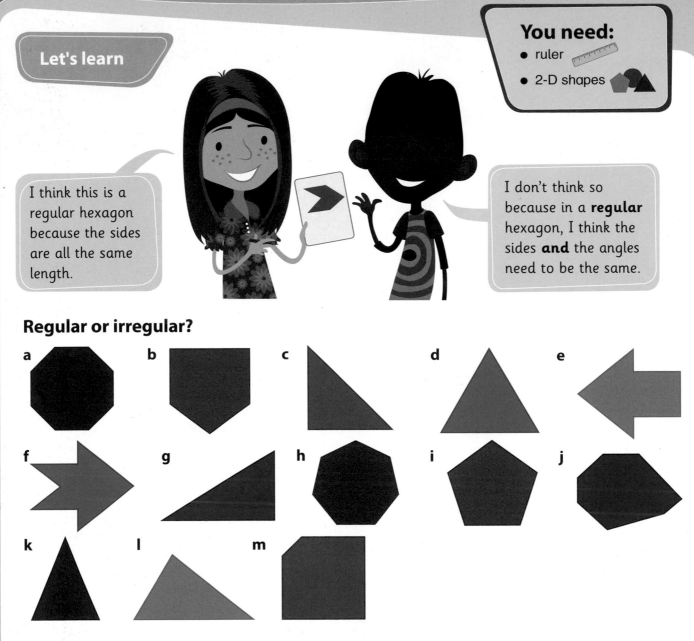

**Let's learn**

**You need:**
- ruler
- 2-D shapes

I think this is a regular hexagon because the sides are all the same length.

I don't think so because in a **regular** hexagon, I think the sides **and** the angles need to be the same.

**Regular or irregular?**

a  b  c  d  e

f  g  h  i  j

k  l  m

A polygon is a **closed** 2-D shape made of straight lines.

If all angles are equal and all sides are equal, then it is a **regular** polygon, otherwise it is **irregular**.

Look at the polygons above. Only **a**, **d**, **h** and **i** are regular.

### Describing properties

Look at the triangles above.

Triangle **c** has 2 acute angles, 2 sides the same length and 1 right angle.

Use angle and side length properties to describe and name some of the other polygons shown.

Teacher's Guide

Before working through the *Textbook*, study page 62 of the *Teacher's Guide* to see how the concepts should be introduced. Read and discuss the page with the children. Provide concrete resources to support exploration.

**1**

### Name and draw.

Name these regular polygons.

Draw an example of an irregular polygon for each one.

Name these irregular polygons.

Draw the regular polygon with the same number of sides.

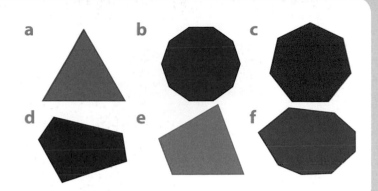

**2**

### Draw.

Draw the 7 different quadrilaterals.

Decide where each one will go in the table.

Some may go in the same section and some sections may stay empty.

|  | No equal sides | 1 pair of equal sides | 2 pairs of equal sides |
|---|---|---|---|
| No parallel sides |  |  |  |
| 1 pair of parallel sides |  |  |  |
| 2 pairs of parallel sides |  |  |  |

Describe a quadrilateral that will fit in the blue section.

Explain why there are no quadrilaterals that fit in some sections.

**3**

### Apply.

If you have 60 metres of fencing, what regular polygon-shaped enclosures can be made that have lengths of whole metres? What lengths would the sides be?

As an example, you could make an equilateral triangle with sides of 20 metres.

**4**

### Investigate.

Look at the shapes that can be made when one regular polygon is moved on top of another.

The red shape is an octagon.          The red shape is a hexagon.

Choose a pair of identical 2-D shapes.

Move 1 shape across the other and then draw, describe and name the new shape.

Repeat with other pairs.

Now try with pairs of different shapes.

Teacher's Guide

See page 63 of the *Teacher's Guide* for ideas of how to guide practice.
Work through each step together as a class to develop children's
conceptual understanding.

**49** ★

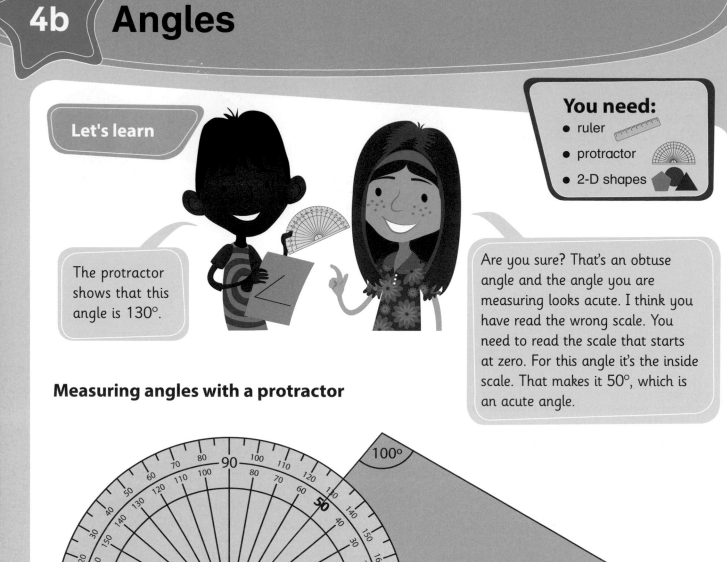

Let's learn

**You need:**
- ruler
- protractor
- 2-D shapes

The protractor shows that this angle is 130°.

Are you sure? That's an obtuse angle and the angle you are measuring looks acute. I think you have read the wrong scale. You need to read the scale that starts at zero. For this angle it's the inside scale. That makes it 50°, which is an acute angle.

## Measuring angles with a protractor

Look at the triangle.

The protractor has been placed with the angle exactly at the vertex.

There are 2 scales, read the one that starts at zero.

Check that you agree it is 50°, not 130°.

What is the sum of the 3 angles?

## Calculating angles without measuring

The angles in a triangle add up to 180°.

Use this fact to calculate the unknown angle.

(You can check your calculation by measuring if you like.)

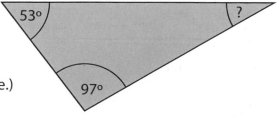

Teacher's Guide

Before working through the *Textbook*, study page 64 of the *Teacher's Guide* to see how the concepts should be introduced. Read and discuss the page with the children. Provide concrete resources to support exploration.

# 1

## Calculate.

Calculate the size of the missing angle or angles.

**a** 72° 44° ?

**b** ? 56° ?

**c** ? ? ?

**d** ? 36°

**e** 74° ? ?

# 2

## Draw.

Draw triangles for each question.

Mark the size of the angles and the equal sides.

**a** 2 isosceles triangles, each with an angle of 70°

**b** 2 isosceles triangles, each with an angle of 34°

**c** 1 right-angled isosceles triangle.

# 3

## Apply.

Work with a partner to draw a sailing boat similar to this one.

Name the angles a, b, c and so on.

Estimate and then measure the angles.

Write them separately and don't show your partner.

Swap drawings. Estimate and measure the angles in each other's boat.

Check your answers. Do you agree?

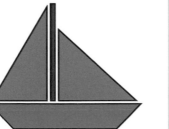

# 4

## Investigate.

Use your knowledge of angles to find the sum of the internal angles of regular polygons.

108° 108° 108° 108° 108°

Can you find a pattern in your answers?

Teacher's Guide

See page 65 of the *Teacher's Guide* for ideas of how to guide practice. Work through each step together as a class to develop children's conceptual understanding.

**51**

**You need:**
- ruler (transparent)
- protractor
- isometric grid paper

I can draw an accurate triangle using a ruler and protractor if I am given 3 measurements.

That might work for some combinations of measurements, but not all of them. Imagine if you just had 3 angles, you wouldn't know if the triangle was tiny or HUGE!

## Drawing angles

This is how you draw an angle of 55° with the vertex on the right:

- First visualise what the finished angle will look like.

- Draw a line.

- Place the origin of the protractor on the right hand end of the line.

- Turn the protractor so that the base line exactly covers the pencil line.

origin

- Mark a small mark at the required angle, ensuring that the correct scale is used.

- Remove the protractor and carefully position the ruler to draw a line from the origin through the mark.

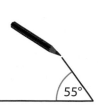

55°

- Check that the angle looks as you expected.

## Drawing triangles

This is how you use a ruler and protractor to draw an equilateral triangle with sides of 4 cm:

- Carefully draw a line exactly 4 cm long.

4 cm

- Place the protractor correctly on one end of the line and measure 60°.

- Mark 60° with a small dot.

- Repeat the 60° angle on the other end of the line.

- Carefully draw the 2 lines to make a triangle.

- Don't worry if the lines are too long at the top.

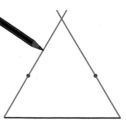

Teacher's Guide

Before working through the *Textbook*, study page 66 of the *Teacher's Guide* to see how the concepts should be introduced. Read and discuss the page with the children. Provide concrete resources to support exploration.

**1**

## Draw.

Draw these angles with the vertex on the left.

**a**   67°

**b**   29°

**c**   102°

Draw these angles with the vertex on the right.

**d**   43°

**e**   126°

**f**   51°

**2**

## Draw.

Use a ruler and protractor to draw these shapes.

**a**   An equilateral triangle with sides of 6 cm.

**b**   An isosceles triangle with a base of 4 cm and 2 angles of 70°. Measure the length of the equal sides in millimetres.

**c**   An accurate hexagon with side length 5 cm.

**3**

## Apply.

Find the combinations of lengths of sides and angle sizes you need to know to draw a triangle accurately using only a ruler and protractor.

**4**

## Investigate.

Use isometric grid paper to find and name as many different polygons as possible.

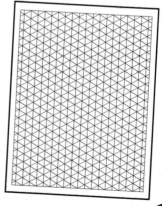

It is possible to find polygons with 3 to 8 sides, and there are several different triangles and quadrilaterals. How many can you find?

Teacher's Guide

See page 67 of the *Teacher's Guide* for ideas of how to guide practice. Work through each step together as a class to develop children's conceptual understanding.

**53** ★

# Making polygons!

Let's play

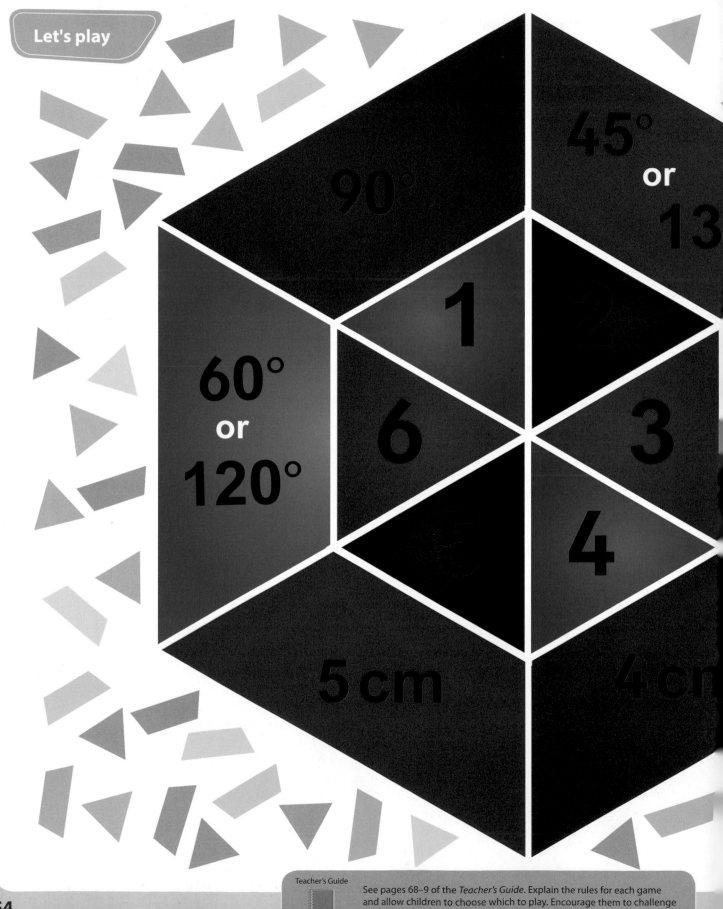

90°

45° or 13

60° or 120°

1

2

6

3

5

4

5 cm

4 cm

Teacher's Guide

See pages 68–9 of the *Teacher's Guide*. Explain the rules for each game and allow children to choose which to play. Encourage them to challenge themselves and practise what they have learnt in the unit.

cm

 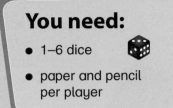
**1 Shape race!**

Play with a partner to build 1 equilateral triangle, 1 isosceles triangle and 1 quadrilateral.

The winner is the first player to make all 3 shapes!

**2 Dozen rolls challenge!**

Build as many polygons as you can from 12 dice rolls. The winner is the player with the most polygons!

**3 Your game**

Now design your own game using the hexagon board.

# And finally ...

**1**

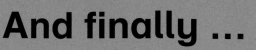

Can you remember all 7 types of quadrilaterals?

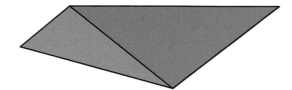

Can you make each type of quadrilateral by putting together 2 triangles?

Draw a table to show your solution, showing clearly the types of triangles you used.

**2**

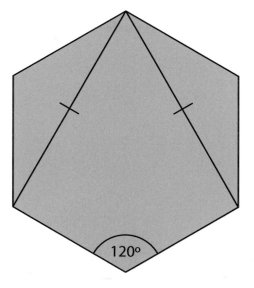

Calculate the missing angles in the diagrams.

Design your own 'missing angle' problem.

Swap your problem with a partner and solve each other's problem.
Discuss your solutions.

Teacher's Guide

See pages 70–1 of the *Teacher's Guide* for guidance on running each task.
Observe children to identify those who have mastered concepts and those who require further consolidation.

**3**

Which of these shapes has parallel sides?

**a**     equilateral triangle

**b**     regular pentagon

**c**     regular octagon

**d**     kite

Think about triangles, quadrilaterals, polygons and angles and write 9 more questions like this with 4 choices in the answer. Try to use all the words in the vocabulary box at least once.

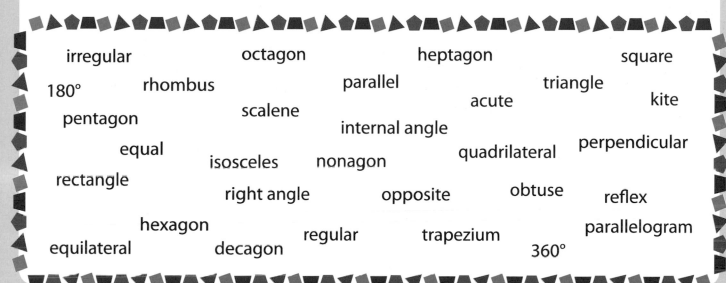

irregular    octagon    heptagon    square

180°    rhombus    parallel    triangle

acute    kite

pentagon    scalene    internal angle

equal    isosceles    nonagon    quadrilateral    perpendicular

rectangle    right angle    opposite    obtuse    reflex

hexagon    regular    trapezium    parallelogram

equilateral    decagon    360°

# Did you know?

Regular polygons have been known for thousands of years. A star pentagon was found on an ancient Greek vase dating from the 7th century BCE!

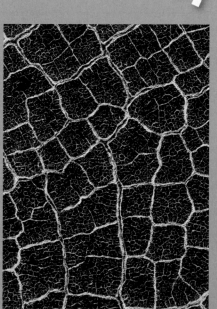

Polygons have recently been found on Mars! Scientists have found polygon-like shapes on the surface of the planet.

# Different types of number

I wonder how many thousands of people were at the match?

Today's Attendance
27 306

Hottest recorded temperature: 56.7°C

Could you work out the difference between these 2 temperatures?

Coldest recorded temperature: −94.7°C

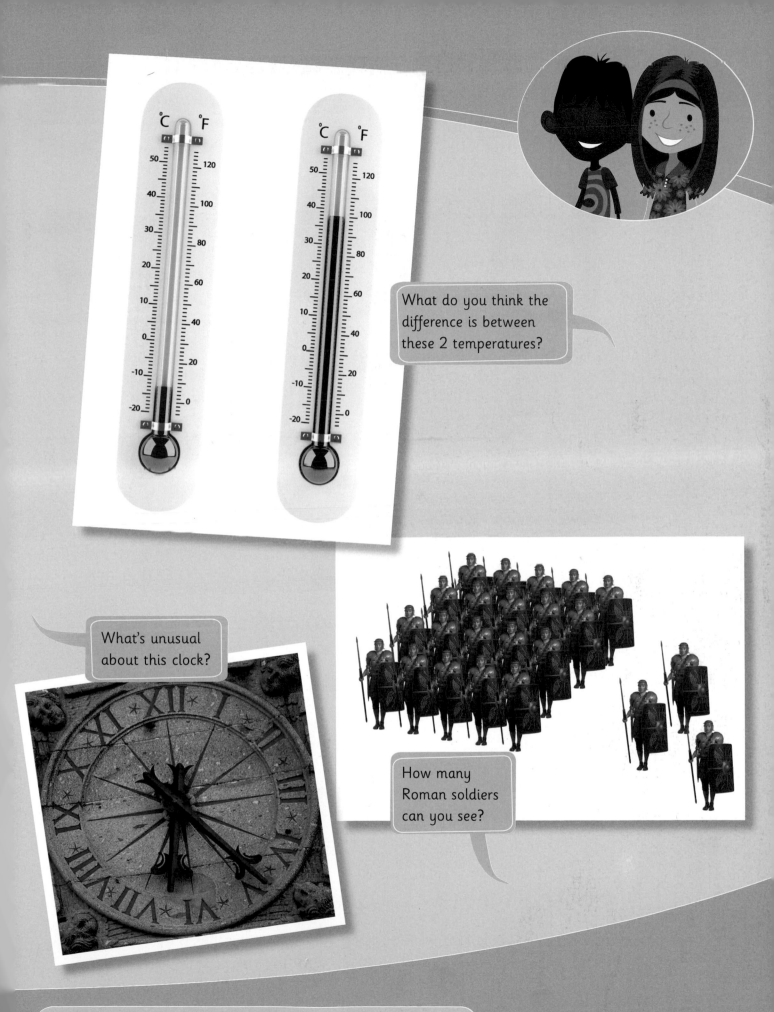

What do you think the difference is between these 2 temperatures?

What's unusual about this clock?

How many Roman soldiers can you see?

Teacher's Guide

Look at the pictures with the children and discuss the questions.
See pages 72–3 of the *Teacher's Guide* for key ideas to draw out.

59

Let's learn

**You need:**
- digit cards
- place-value grid
- place-value cards
- sand
- small plastic bags
- scales

I think that 210 thousand and 87 is written like this.

21 087    210 087

That is 21 thousand and 87! It should be written like this. You missed out the place holder for the hundreds.

## Place holders

| 100 000 | 10 000 | 1 000 | 100 | 10 | 1 |
|---------|--------|-------|-----|-----|---|
| 2 | 1 | 0 | 0 | 8 | 7 |
| 3 | 4 | 0 | 5 | 0 | 5 |
| 2 | 0 | 5 | 0 | 0 | 6 |

Zero is the symbol we use as a place holder when a column does not have a quantity.

What are the numbers in the table? What would they be without the zero place holders?

Without place holders, the numbers would be much smaller!

## Comparing numbers

$$100\,450 \; > \; 100\,275 \qquad\qquad 235\,098 \; < \; 235\,260$$

To order these numbers look at the position where the digits are different. These both have the same thousands digits, so look at the hundreds and find the largest of these.

$$120\,365 + 100\,213 \; = \; 200\,451 + 20\,127$$

The equals symbol shows that what is on one side is the same as on the other. Is this number statement correct?

Teacher's Guide

Before working through the *Textbook*, study page 74 of the *Teacher's Guide* to see how the concepts should be introduced. Read and discuss the page with the children. Provide concrete resources to support exploration.

## 1

### Create.

Use these digits to make up as many 4-digit numbers as you can.

6    9    5    0

Now order them from largest to smallest.

## 2

### Write.

Write down what the place holders are in these numbers.

| | | | | |
|---|---|---|---|---|
| a | 508 | d | 84 350 |
| b | 1065 | e | 105 487 |
| c | 20 575 | f | 240 067 |

Now write the numbers in words.

## 3

### Measure.

Weigh these amounts of sand and put each in a small plastic bag:

- 750 g
- 250 g
- 500 g

Make up all the greater than and less than statements that you can.

Now make up all the statements you can with the equals symbol.

## 4

### Think.

I think that the equals symbol means that there is an answer on the other side of a calculation.

Explain why Amy is incorrect.

Teacher's Guide

See page 75 of the *Teacher's Guide* for ideas of how to guide practice. Work through each step together as a class to develop children's conceptual understanding.

61 ★

**Let's learn**

**You need:**
- number square
- clock faces

I think 51 must be written in Roman numerals like this.

V is 5 and I is 1, so that's 6! It should be 50 and 1 which is written like this.

VI LI

## Roman numerals

| | | | | | | | | | |
|---|---|---|---|---|---|---|---|---|---|
| **Ones** | I<br>1 | II<br>2 | III<br>3 | IV<br>4 | V<br>5 | VI<br>6 | VII<br>7 | VIII<br>8 | IX<br>9 |
| **Tens** | X<br>10 | XX<br>20 | XXX<br>30 | XL<br>40 | L<br>50 | LX<br>60 | LXX<br>70 | LXXX<br>80 | XC<br>90 |
| **Hundreds** | C<br>100 | CC<br>200 | CCC<br>300 | CD<br>400 | D<br>500 | DC<br>600 | DCC<br>700 | DCCC<br>800 | CM<br>900 |
| **Thousands** | M<br>1000 | MM<br>2000 | MMM<br>3000 | $\overline{\text{IV}}$<br>4000 | $\overline{\text{V}}$<br>5000 | $\overline{\text{VI}}$<br>6000 | $\overline{\text{VII}}$<br>7000 | $\overline{\text{VIII}}$<br>8000 | $\overline{\text{IX}}$<br>9000 |

Use the table to make up some numbers using Roman numerals. Write them and our numbers as equivalence statements, e.g. XVI = 16 .

Roman numerals are used to show the year films were made, so 2015 is written as MMXV.

Choose another year to write in Roman numerals.

## Time

Roman numerals can be used to show the hour numbers on some clocks.

Can you think of when you have seen a Roman numeral clock?

Make up some digital times. Record these using Roman numerals.

Teacher's Guide

Before working through the *Textbook*, study page 78 of the *Teacher's Guide* to see how the concepts should be introduced. Read and discuss the page with the children. Provide concrete resources to support exploration.

## 1

### Write.

Write these numbers in Roman numerals.

**a**    Your age      **d**    456

**b**    13             **e**    705

**c**    24             **f**    995

Now explain how you did this.

## 2

### Write.

Write these Roman numerals in our numbers.

**a**    XV        **d**    CDLX

**b**    XXIX      **e**    DCXIV

**c**    LVII       **f**    CMLV

Now explain how you worked these out.

## 3

### Draw.

Draw clock faces to show these times.

**a**    The minute hand is on II and the hour hand is just past the VIII.

**b**    The minute hand is on XI and the hour hand is just before VI.

**c**    The minute hand is on IV and the hour hand is just past XII.

**d**    The minute hand is on IX and the hour hand is just before V.

Now label the times using digital time.

## 4

### Play.

Make a cube and number the faces with Roman numerals from 1 to 6. This is your dice. Play this game with a partner:

- Take turns to throw both dice.
- Find the total of the 2 numbers that you can see.
- Do this 10 times.
- Total your score – using Roman numerals!

> If you've got the highest total you win!

Teacher's Guide

See page 79 of the *Teacher's Guide* for ideas of how to guide practice. Work through each step together as a class to develop children's conceptual understanding.

65

# A mixture of numbers

Let's play

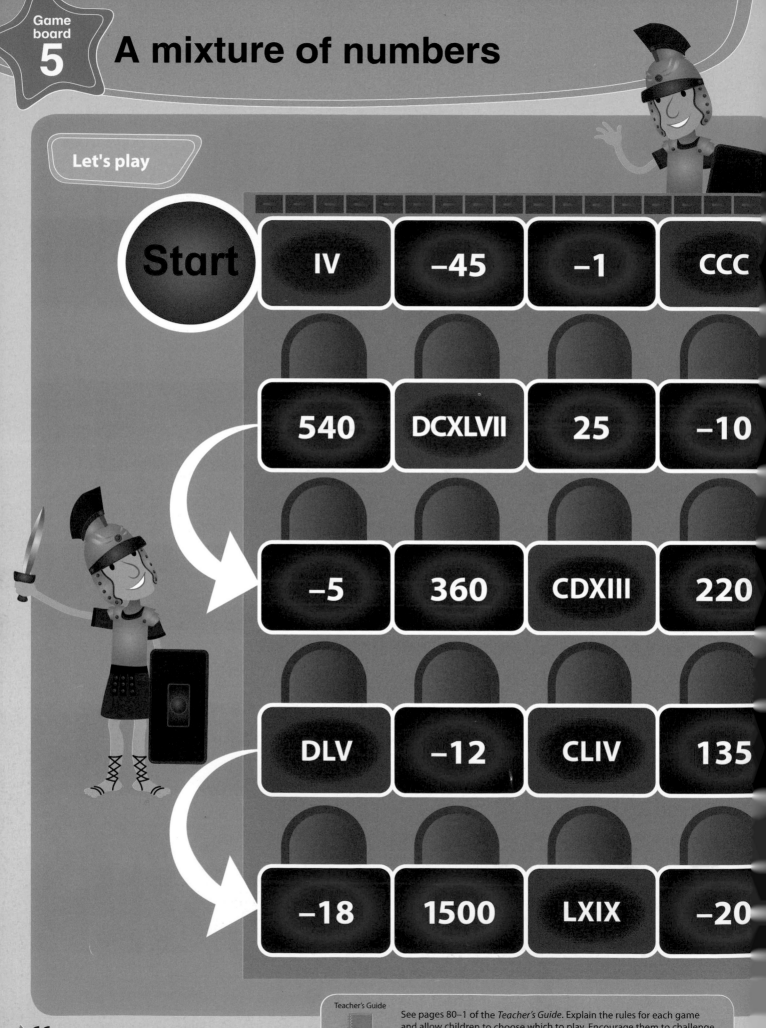

Start

| IV | –45 | –1 | CCC |

| 540 | DCXLVII | 25 | –10 |

| –5 | 360 | CDXIII | 220 |

| DLV | –12 | CLIV | 135 |

| –18 | 1500 | LXIX | –20 |

Teacher's Guide

See pages 80–1 of the *Teacher's Guide*. Explain the rules for each game and allow children to choose which to play. Encourage them to challenge themselves and practise what they have learnt in the unit.

**You need:**
- 1–6 dice
- counters
- paper and pencils

**1** **Highest total**

Throw the dice and work your way around the board, totalling the numbers you land on. The highest total wins!

**2** **Four in a row**

If you throw an even number put a counter on 1 of the squares. Try to get 4 counters in a row to give the highest score possible!

**3** **Your game**

Design your own game. Explain the rules and play with a partner.

# And finally ...

**1**

Mercury is a planet that has no atmosphere so it can't hold heat like the Earth. The side that faces the sun is very hot and the side away from the sun is very cold.

If the hottest side is 158°C and the coldest side is −115°C what is the temperature difference?

Explain how you worked out the answer.

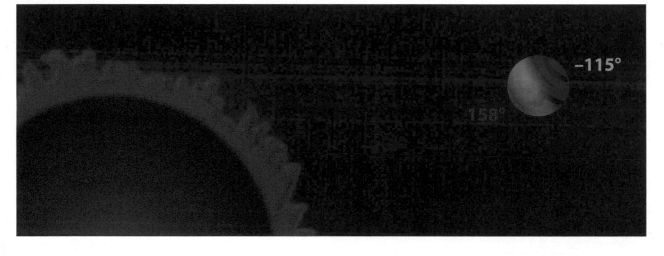

**2**

Write each of these numbers in words:

a    350 127

b    207 549

c    134 083

d    405 304

e    600 200

f    420 060

Beside each number explain what the place holders represent.

Now explain in writing or to your teacher the position of each digit and what its value is.

Teacher's Guide     See pages 82–3 of the *Teacher's Guide* for guidance on running each task. Observe children to identify those who have mastered concepts and those who require further consolidation.

★68

**3**

Write these numbers as Roman numerals:

a    16

b    58

c    81

d    135

e    649

f    967

> Remember to partition the numbers into tens and ones, or hundreds, tens and ones and to convert each part.

Write these Roman numerals using our number system:

g    VII

h    CIX

i    DCCLV

j    CDXXII

k    CMXCIX

l    MCXI

> Look back at the table on page 64 if you need to.

# Did you know?

> The Romans didn't have a symbol for zero. They simply used the symbols for the thousands, hundreds, tens and ones. If there was nothing in the tens, it was ignored!

> So 301 would have been written CCCI, with nothing to show that there are no tens!

A·D MCMXXII

# Mental and written methods for addition and subtraction

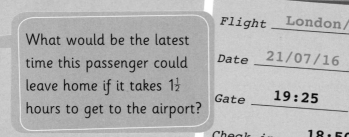

What would be the latest time this passenger could leave home if it takes $1\frac{1}{2}$ hours to get to the airport?

**Air ticket**

Flight ___London/Amsterdam___

Date ___21/07/16___  Time **19:55**

Gate ___19:25___

Check-in ___18:50___

Seat ___J44___

**Air ticket**

Name ___M.Aths___

Flight ___Lon/Ams___

Date ___21/07/16___

Time ___19:55___

Gate ___19:25___

Seat ___J44___

The luggage is over the weight limit! I wonder what the passenger can do?

MD FARIS

**Maximum weight
per person
20 kg**

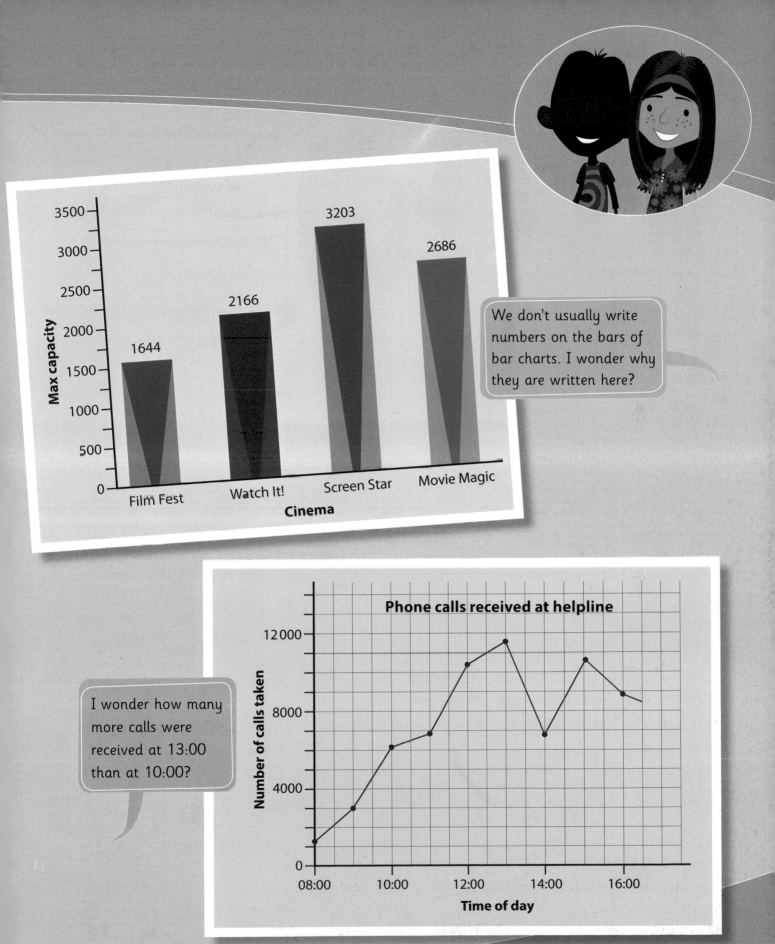

We don't usually write numbers on the bars of bar charts. I wonder why they are written here?

I wonder how many more calls were received at 13:00 than at 10:00?

Teacher's Guide

Look at the pictures with the children and discuss the questions.
See pages 84–5 of the *Teacher's Guide* for key ideas to draw out.

71

**Let's learn**

We should always use a written method when we add or subtract larger numbers.

No, that's not true. We need to look at the numbers and then decide which is the most efficient.

**You need:**
- number lines
- calculator

## Totals

$1350 + 760 = ?$

Would you choose a mental or written method to find the total? Why?

The mental number line or a sequencing method would be helpful as 1350 and 760 are multiples of 10.

$$\begin{array}{r} 1350 \\ + \phantom{0}760 \\ \hline 2110 \\ \tiny{1\phantom{0}1} \end{array}$$

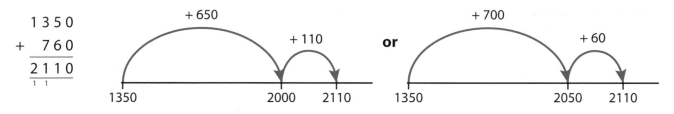

+ 650    + 110

1350    2000   2110

**or**

+ 700    + 60

1350    2050   2110

Try the calculation using the sequencing method.

Which method would you use for $1.35 + 0.76$?

## Subtraction as 'finding the difference'

You must also choose the best method to solve subtraction calculations.

What do you notice about these two methods?

$$\begin{array}{r} \overset{12}{\cancel{1}}\overset{\phantom{0}1}{3}50 \\ - \phantom{0}760 \\ \hline 590 \end{array}$$

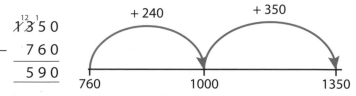

+ 240    + 350

760    1000    1350

It is easy to use counting on to find the difference between two values that are close together, e.g. 1426 and 1485.

It is also a good method for numbers that are close to boundaries, e.g. 8009 and 3950.

Try finding the difference between 1.35 and 0.76.

Will you use the number line and the counting-on method or a written method? Why?

Teacher's Guide

Before working through the *Textbook*, study page 86 of the *Teacher's Guide* to see how the concepts should be introduced. Read and discuss the page with the children. Provide concrete resources to support exploration.

## 1

### Answer these.

Choose a mental method for 2 of these calculations and a written method for the other 2.
Be prepared to explain your choices.

a    3749 + 2583

c    6518 + 3789

b    4750 + 1900

d    12 895 + 10 105

Choose the counting-on method for 2 of these calculations and the written method for the other 2. Be prepared to explain your choices.

e    3845 – 3799

g    7012 – 2975

f    6387 – 3254

h    18 765 – 5248

## 2

### Solve these.

Use rounding to make an estimate first.
Then use the sequencing method to solve these calculations.

a    3145 g + 2310 g

c    3.6 kg + 4.7 kg

b    4878 g + 925 g

d    1.68 kg + 2.12 kg

## 3

### Apply.

Choose a mental or a written method to find the total or differences.

a    495 g + 2 kg

Remember to check that both units of measurement are the same before calculating!

b    3.75 kg + 768 g

c    3.5 kg + 400 g + 150 g

d    5 kg – 1788 g

e    17.55 kg – 4.82 kg

f    3250 g – 2.68 kg

Now use a calculator to check each of your calculations.

## 4

### Think.

Write a 'difference' calculation about mass where it is better to use a mental method.

Now write another…
and another…
and another.

Explain why you have chosen these calculations.

Now write a calculation where it would be better to use a written method.

Teacher's Guide

See page 87 of the *Teacher's Guide* for ideas of how to guide practice.
Work through each step together as a class to develop children's
conceptual understanding.

**73** ★

# Don't forget to check!

**Let's learn**

**You need:**

- place-value counters
- number lines
- clocks
- Base 10 apparatus
- number rods

*I know my calculations are correct because I always do them twice.*

*But you could make the same mistake twice! You should use the inverse or a different method to check.*

## Calculating and checking time intervals

The bus takes 34 minutes to travel from the park to the cinema.

| Bus timetable | |
| --- | --- |
| **Park** | **Cinema** |
| 14:52 | 15:26 |

Number lines are useful when working with time. You don't have to think about columns. You can use a counting-back method to check.

+ 8 minutes  + 26 minutes        − 8 minutes  − 26 minutes

14:52    15:00    15:26    14:52    15:00    15:26

## Solving problems and checking answers

| Cinema | Film Fest | Watch It! | Screen Star | Movie Magic |
| --- | --- | --- | --- | --- |
| **Max capacity** | 1644 | 2166 | 3203 | 2686 |

This bar model represents the difference between the number of seats at 2 cinemas.

Which cinemas are they?

Find the difference and complete this number statement.

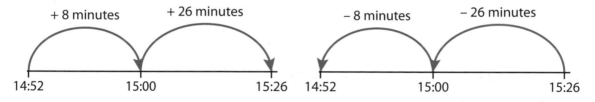

| 3203 | |
| --- | --- |
| 2166 | ? |

_____ has [ ] more seats than _____

Use an addition calculation to check your working.

2166  +  ?  =  3203   What method will you use?

Teacher's Guide

Before working through the *Textbook*, study page 88 of the *Teacher's Guide* to see how the concepts should be introduced. Read and discuss the page with the children. Provide concrete resources to support exploration.

**1**

## Calculate.

Calculate these time intervals.

**a**    9:45 a.m. and 1:20 p.m.

**b**    Noon and 17:30

**c**    10:26 and 13:09

**d**    13:46 and 19:15

**e**    18:22 and midnight

**f**    07:12 and 16:15

**2**

## Answer these.

Find the total number of seats at the cinemas.

**a**    Film Fest and Screen Star

**b**    Movie Magic and Watch It!

**c**    Watch It! and Screen Star and Movie Magic

**d**    All 4 cinemas

**e**    Write a different calculation to check your answers.

> You may wish to use place-value counters.

**3**

## Solve the problem.

The total amount of money taken on one day at Movie Magic was £19 254.

£16 116 was taken in ticket sales and the remainder on sales of snacks and drinks.

How much was taken on snacks and drinks? Begin by drawing a bar model to represent the problem.

Write a different calculation to check your answer.

**4**

## Investigate.

A 3-digit number

A 4-digit number

The sum of these 2 numbers rounds to 2300 to the nearest hundred.

The difference between these 2 numbers rounds to 500 to the nearest hundred.

Find at least 3 ways to make this true.

Teacher's Guide

See page 89 of the *Teacher's Guide* for ideas of how to guide practice. Work through each step together as a class to develop children's conceptual understanding.

75

# A wise choice...

Let's play

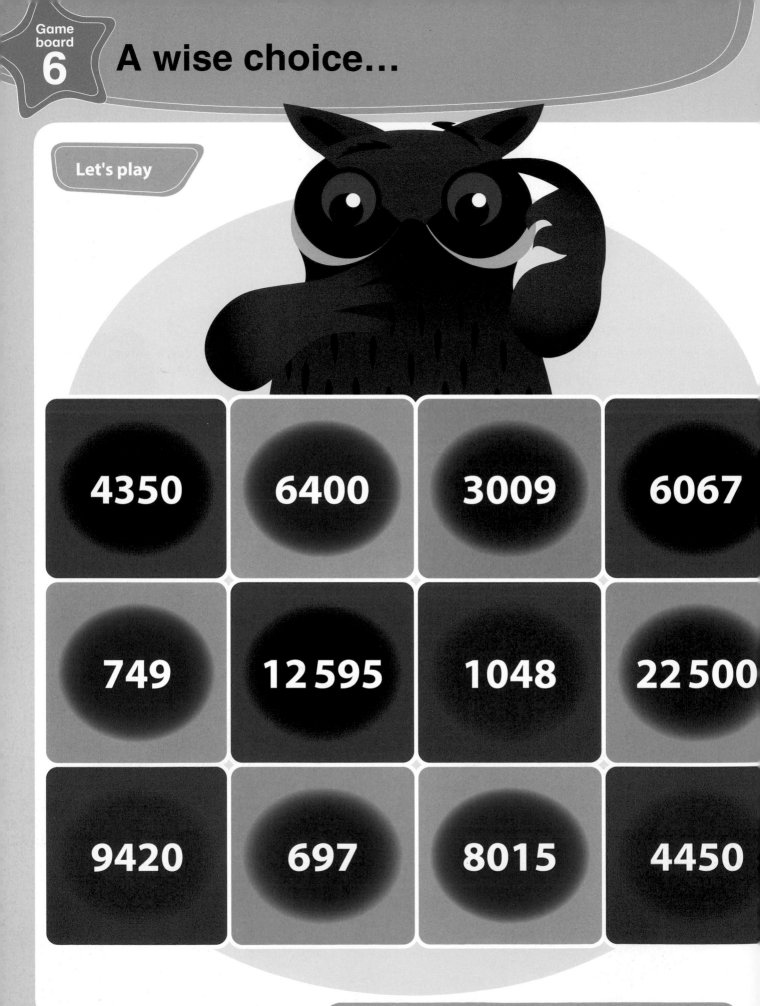

| | | | |
|---|---|---|---|
| 4350 | 6400 | 3009 | 6067 |
| 749 | 12 595 | 1048 | 22 500 |
| 9420 | 697 | 8015 | 4450 |

Teacher's Guide

See pages 90–1 of the *Teacher's Guide*. Explain the rules for each game and allow children to choose which to play. Encourage them to challenge themselves and practise what they have learnt in the unit.

**Game 1**

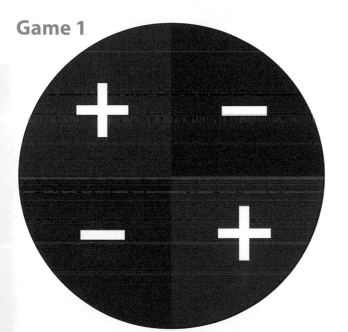

**Game 2**

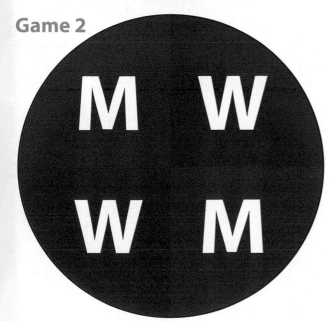

**1** **Pick a number**
Try to solve calculations correctly and cover as many numbers as possible!

**2** **Four in a row**
Use both spinners to play. Will you use a mental or written method?

**3** **Your game**
Design your own game using the gameboard.

# And finally …

**Let's review**

**1**

Theo has completed some calculations.
Are his answers correct?

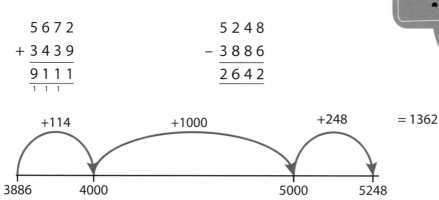

$$
\begin{array}{r}
5\,6\,7\,2 \\
+\ 3\,4\,3\,9 \\
\hline
9\,1\,1\,1 \\
\scriptstyle 1\ \ 1\ \ 1
\end{array}
\qquad
\begin{array}{r}
5\,2\,4\,8 \\
-\ 3\,8\,8\,6 \\
\hline
2\,6\,4\,2
\end{array}
$$

+114      +1000      +248      = 1362

3886    4000              5000    5248

Check his working and correct any mistakes.

What would you say to Theo to help him with
other calculations like this?

**2**

What different methods can Amy use to answer these?

**a**    11 254 – 5500

**b**    12 465 + 1535

**c**    9468 + 999

**d**    8964 – 7890

**e**    Pick pairs of numbers to make up addition and subtraction
calculations. These should be suitable for using a mental method.

I wonder if I can use a
mental method for each
of these calculations?

13 465    8000    5750    2465    3009    2250    11 002

Teacher's Guide

See pages 92–3 of the *Teacher's Guide* for guidance on running each task.
Observe children to identify those who have mastered concepts and those who
require further consolidation.

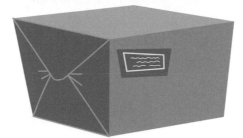

**3**

The difference between the mass of 2 parcels is approximately 3.5 kg.

What could each parcel weigh?

Find an easy and a hard solution.

I think that 2 parcels could weigh 4.6 kg and 1700 g. Do you agree?

# Did you know?

The Ancient Egyptians used these symbols for addition and subtraction. The legs walking forwards represent addition and the legs walking backwards represent subtraction!

I found out that the equals sign (=) was invented in 1557 by Welsh mathematician Robert Recorde. He was fed up with writing 'is equal to' in his equations! He chose the two lines because 'no two things can be more equal'.

# Fractions, decimals and percentages

I wonder what fraction these slices are of the whole pies?

Once the boy has eaten that piece of chocolate, can you work out what fraction of the chocolate will be left?

3.25 kg
£1.20/kg
£3.90

1.5 kg
£2.00/kg
£3.00

2.75 kg
£0.70/kg
£1.92

I wonder if you could show the masses of these different foods using fractions?

What does 6.9 g of carbohydrate mean?

| Nutrition information | | | |
|---|---|---|---|
| **Typical values** | Per 100g | Per $\frac{1}{4}$ pot | % based on GDA for women |
| **Energy** | 256 kJ **61 kcal** | 320 kJ **76 kcal** | **3.8%** |
| **Protein** | 4.9g | 6.1g | 13.6% |
| **Carbohydrate** of which **sugars** of which starch | 6.9g 6.9g nil | 8.6g **8.6g** nil | 3.7% 9.6% - |
| **Fat** of which **saturates** mono-unsaturates polyunsaturates | 1.5g 0.9g 0.4g nil | 1.9g 1.1g 0.5g nil | 2.7% 5.5% - - |
| **Fibre** | **nil** | **nil** | **nil** |
| **Salt** of which sodium | 0.2g trace | **0.3g** 0.1g | 5.0% 4.2% |
| **Vitamnins and minerals** | | Recommended daily amount | % of RDA |
| **Calcium** | **168mg** | **210mg** | **26%** |

Teacher's Guide
Look at the pictures with the children and discuss the questions.
See pages 94–5 of the *Teacher's Guide* for key ideas to draw out.

81 ☆

# Comparing and ordering fractions

Let's learn

I think that $\frac{1}{8}$ is bigger than $\frac{1}{4}$ because 8 is bigger than 4.

No it isn't! $\frac{1}{8}$ is smaller than $\frac{1}{4}$. To find $\frac{1}{8}$ you divide something into 8 parts and to find $\frac{1}{4}$ you divide it into 4 parts. So the 8 parts will be smaller than the 4.

## Comparing fractions

Look at the denominators. These tell you how many parts there are. The higher the denominator the smaller the fraction.

Which of the fractions here are smaller than $\frac{1}{2}$?

Which are bigger than $\frac{7}{16}$?

Make up some number statements using the fractions and the symbols >, < and =.

## Ordering fractions

When the numerators and denominators are different you can make them into equivalent fractions.

Look at the fraction wall. How many twelfths are equivalent to $\frac{2}{3}$ and $\frac{5}{6}$? Now order $\frac{2}{3}$, $\frac{5}{6}$ and $\frac{5}{12}$.

Teacher's Guide

Before working through the *Textbook*, study page 96 of the *Teacher's Guide* to see how the concepts should be introduced. Read and discuss the page with the children. Provide concrete resources to support exploration.

**1**

## Compare.

Write number statements using the symbols >, < and =.

a   $\frac{3}{4}$ ▢ $\frac{7}{8}$

d   $\frac{1}{6}$ ▢ $\frac{5}{9}$

b   $\frac{1}{2}$ ▢ $\frac{7}{16}$

e   $\frac{3}{8}$ ▢ $\frac{7}{16}$

c   $\frac{2}{3}$ ▢ $\frac{8}{12}$

f   $\frac{3}{9}$ ▢ $\frac{1}{3}$

**2**

## Make.

Throw a pair of dice. Use the numbers to make a fraction. The smallest number you throw is the numerator. The largest is the denominator.

Do this 5 times.

Now order the fractions from largest to smallest.

**3**

## Measure.

Measure out these amounts of sand into plastic bags.
Order the masses from smallest to largest.

a   $1\frac{1}{2}$ kg   $1\frac{1}{4}$ kg   $1\frac{1}{10}$ kg   $1\frac{1}{5}$ kg   $1\frac{1}{8}$ kg

b   $5\frac{1}{3}$ kg   $5\frac{1}{2}$ kg   $5\frac{1}{9}$ kg   $5\frac{1}{6}$ kg   $5\frac{1}{12}$ kg

Fill 2 or more 2-litre bottles with these amounts.
Order their volumes from greatest to smallest.

c   $2\frac{1}{4}$ l   $2\frac{1}{5}$ l   $2\frac{1}{2}$ l   $2\frac{1}{10}$ l   $2\frac{1}{3}$ l

d   $4\frac{3}{4}$ l   $4\frac{1}{2}$ l   $4\frac{1}{4}$ l   $4\frac{9}{10}$ l   $4\frac{1}{8}$ l

**4**

## Think.

So, the larger the denominator the larger the fraction!

Is this always incorrect?

Teacher's Guide

See page 97 of the *Teacher's Guide* for ideas of how to guide practice.
Work through each step together as a class to develop children's
conceptual understanding.

**83** ★

# Improper fractions and mixed numbers

**Let's learn**

$\frac{9}{5}$ can't be a fraction because it is bigger than one whole.

Yes it is. It's called an improper fraction. We can turn it into a mixed number which would be $1\frac{4}{5}$.

## Improper fractions

An improper fraction is a fraction that is more than one whole. The numerator is a higher number than the denominator.

What is the same about these pictures?

What is different?

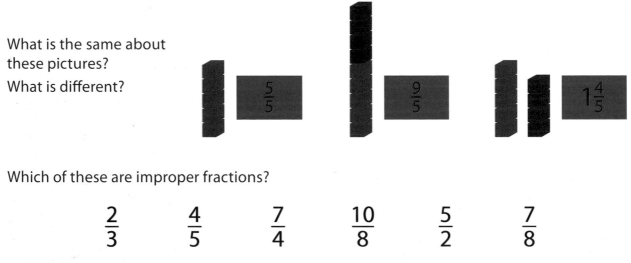

$\frac{5}{5}$     $\frac{9}{5}$     $1\frac{4}{5}$

Which of these are improper fractions?

$$\frac{2}{3} \qquad \frac{4}{5} \qquad \frac{7}{4} \qquad \frac{10}{8} \qquad \frac{5}{2} \qquad \frac{7}{8}$$

Explain how you know to your partner.

## Mixed numbers

A mixed number is a mixture of whole numbers and fractions. These can also be shown as improper fractions.

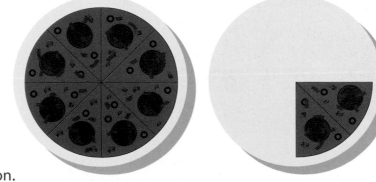

Write the amount of pizza shown here as a mixed number.

Now write it as an improper fraction.

**1**

**Write.**

Write these improper fractions as mixed numbers.

a $\frac{13}{10}$    b $\frac{9}{4}$    c $\frac{12}{8}$    d $\frac{14}{5}$    e $\frac{7}{2}$    f $\frac{14}{3}$

**2**

**Write.**

Write these mixed numbers as improper fractions.

a $3\frac{1}{3}$    b $2\frac{4}{5}$    c $4\frac{5}{6}$    d $5\frac{3}{4}$    e $8\frac{1}{2}$    f $12\frac{7}{8}$

**3**

**Apply.**

Write these lengths.
Circle any that are improper fractions.

a $\frac{1}{2}$ m   $\frac{12}{10}$ m   $\frac{4}{5}$ m   $\frac{6}{5}$ m   $\frac{7}{4}$ m

b $\frac{11}{10}$ cm   $\frac{6}{5}$ cm   $\frac{1}{2}$ cm   $\frac{3}{2}$ cm   $\frac{7}{10}$ cm

Measure and cut all the lengths from strips of paper.
Stick strips together for the metre measurement.
Compare pairs of lengths using the symbols > and <.

Change these lengths to mixed numbers.

c $\frac{5}{2}$ m   $\frac{6}{5}$ m   $\frac{15}{10}$ m   $\frac{25}{20}$ m   $\frac{16}{5}$ m

d $\frac{12}{5}$ cm   $\frac{9}{2}$ cm   $\frac{21}{10}$ cm   $\frac{18}{5}$ cm   $\frac{13}{2}$ cm

Measure and cut all the lengths from strips of paper,
you may need to stick strips together for the metre
measurement. Compare pairs of lengths using the
symbols > and <.

**4**

**Think.**

Use these digits
to make as many
improper fractions as
you can. They should
be thousandths.

Now write them as
proper fractions.

Teacher's Guide    See page 99 of the *Teacher's Guide* for ideas of how to guide practice.
Work through each step together as a class to develop children's
conceptual understanding.

**85** ⭐

# Equivalences

Let's learn

Decimals aren't fractions. Fractions always need denominators and numerators. Decimals don't have those.

Yes, decimals are fractions. They are called decimal fractions. They show parts of a whole just like other fractions.

**You need:**
- place-value grids (thousands to hundredths)
- digit cards
- coloured counters
- scales
- Base 10 apparatus

## Decimal fraction equivalences

| 1000 | 100 | 10 | 1 | . | 10th | 100th | 1000th |
|------|-----|----|----|---|------|-------|--------|
| 6 | 7 | 3 | 4 | . | 2 | 5 | |

Make this number on your place-value grid.
Explain to your partner what each digit stands for.

Decimal fractions are fractions written in a different form. In the grid above the digit 2 is in the tenths position. Its value is 0.2 or $\frac{2}{10}$. The digit 5 is in the hundredths position. Its value is 0.05 or $\frac{5}{100}$.

Write some decimal numbers and convert them to their equivalent fractions.

## Thousandths

If you put an 8 in the thousandths position of the grid it has the value of 0.008 or $\frac{8}{1000}$. The whole decimal part to the number is then 0.258 or $\frac{258}{1000}$. One thousandth is 100 times smaller than one tenth and 10 times smaller than one hundredth.

| 1000 | 100 | 10 | 1 | . | 10th | 100th | 1000th |
|------|-----|----|----|---|------|-------|--------|
| 6 | 7 | 3 | 4 | . | 2 | 5 | 8 |

Write some thousandths numbers and convert them to their equivalent fractions.

Teacher's Guide

Before working through the *Textbook*, study page 100 of the *Teacher's Guide* to see how the concepts should be introduced. Read and discuss the page with the children. Provide concrete resources to support exploration.

**1**

**Write.**

Write these decimal numbers as fractions.

a    1.2          b    2.5          c    3.28          d    6.35          e    12.76          f    15.275

Explain how you did this.
Now reduce the fractions.

**2**

**Write.**

Write these mixed numbers as decimal numbers.

a    $2\frac{3}{10}$          b    $6\frac{9}{10}$          c    $7\frac{7}{10}$          d    $4\frac{12}{100}$          e    $6\frac{86}{100}$          f    $28\frac{255}{1000}$

Explain how you worked these out.

**3**

**Apply.**

Milo, Freya, Jenny and Freddie have 6 pizzas to share.

a    They share them equally. Write the amount of pizza that each has as a mixed number and an improper fraction.

b    Amy also wants to share the pizzas. How much does each have now?

c    How much do they each have if James also wants a share?

d    What about if Emma also wants a share?

**4**

**Think.**

I think that 3 kg and 75 g can be written as 3.75 kg.

Explain why Amy is incorrect.

Teacher's Guide
See page 101 of the *Teacher's Guide* for ideas of how to guide practice.
Work through each step together as a class to develop children's
conceptual understanding.

**87** ⭐

# Percentages

**Let's learn**

25 per cent must be written like this. The percentage is the denominator.

No it's not! A percentage is a special fraction. The denominator is always 100. So 25 per cent is written like this.

**You need:**
- strips of paper
- money
- scales
- measuring jug

| 1% | 2% | 3% | 4% | 5% | 6% | 7% | 8% | 9% | 10% |
|----|----|----|----|----|----|----|----|----|-----|
| 11% | 12% | 13% | 14% | 15% | 16% | 17% | 18% | 19% | 20% |
| 21% | 22% | 23% | 24% | 25% | 26% | 27% | 28% | 29% | 30% |
| 31% | 32% | 33% | 34% | 35% | 36% | 37% | 38% | 39% | 40% |
| 41% | 42% | 43% | 44% | 45% | 46% | 47% | 48% | 49% | 50% |
| 51% | 52% | 53% | 54% | 55% | 56% | 57% | 58% | 59% | 60% |
| 61% | 62% | 63% | 64% | 65% | 66% | 67% | 68% | 69% | 70% |
| 71% | 72% | 73% | 74% | 75% | 76% | 77% | 78% | 79% | 80% |
| 81% | 82% | 83% | 84% | 85% | 86% | 87% | 88% | 89% | 90% |
| 91% | 92% | 93% | 94% | 95% | 96% | 97% | 98% | 99% | 100% |

## Percentages

Percentages are special fractions. They are always hundredths.

10 per cent is 10 parts out of 100 or $\frac{10}{100}$

50 per cent is 50 parts out of 100 or $\frac{50}{100}$.

To work out a percentage, find 10 per cent first, then double, halve, multiply or divide by 10 and add or subtract. Look at this example for different percentages of £240:

## Percentage equivalences

Place a strip of paper across the first row of the percentages table to cover 10 per cent.

This is the same as $\frac{10}{100}$ which is equivalent to $\frac{1}{10}$ and the decimal 0.1.

Place strips of paper over the next 4 rows. You have covered half the grid. What is that as a percentage?

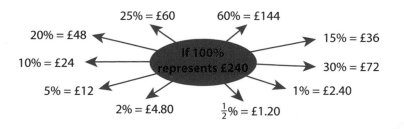

25% = £60    60% = £144
20% = £48    15% = £36
10% = £24    If 100% represents £240    30% = £72
5% = £12     1% = £2.40
2% = £4.80   $\frac{1}{2}$% = £1.20

**Teacher's Guide**

Before working through the *Textbook*, study page 102 of the *Teacher's Guide* to see how the concepts should be introduced. Read and discuss the page with the children. Provide concrete resources to support exploration.

**1**

**Answer these.**

Write these percentages as hundredths.

a    10%            c    70%            e    64%

b    30%            d    45%            f    82%

Explain how you know this.
Now reduce the fractions that you have made.

**2**

**Answer these.**

Change these percentages to fractions and decimals.

a    50%            c    25%            e    96%

b    30%            d    65%            f    7%

**3**

**Solve.**

a    10% of £50

b    20% of £80

c    70% of £60

d    15% of £200

e    35% of £150

f    84% of £360

Explain how you worked these out.
Draw how you could make these
amounts using the fewest number
of coins and notes.

**4**

**Think.**

Which would you rather see in your bedroom?

a    35% of 50 spiders

b    40% of 40 spiders

c    60% of 30 spiders?

Make sure you explain
your reasons clearly.

Make up another 'would you rather' problem
… and another
… and another!

Teacher's Guide    See page 103 of the *Teacher's Guide* for ideas of how to guide practice.
Work through each step together as a class to develop children's
conceptual understanding.

# Fraction fun!

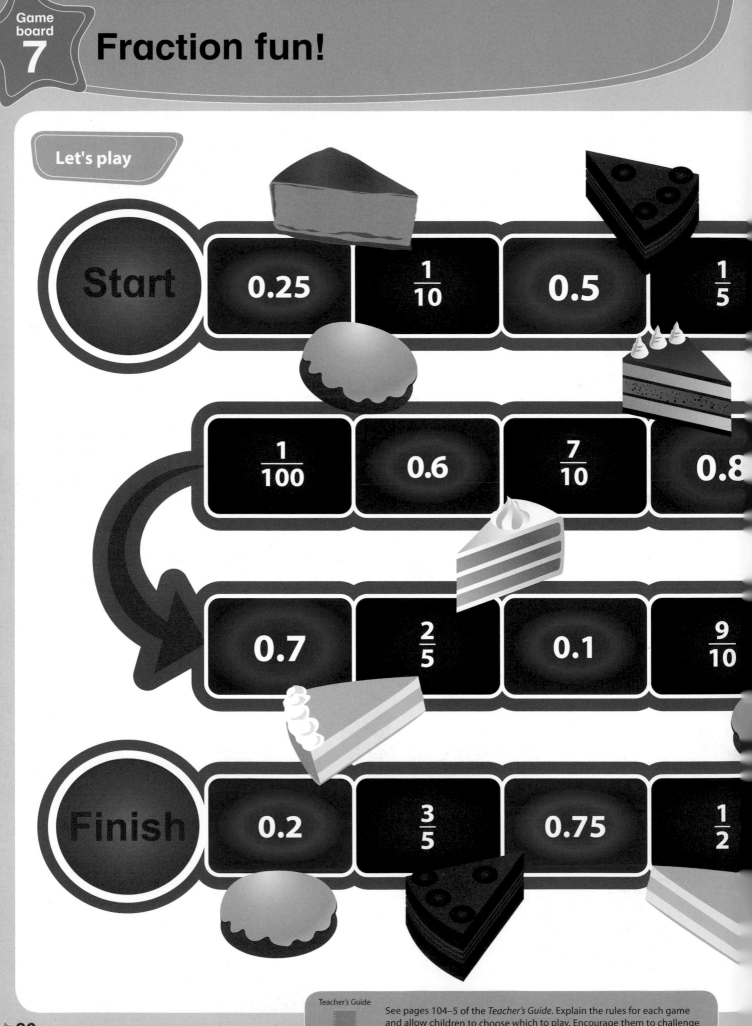

Let's play

Start
0.25
$\frac{1}{10}$
0.5
$\frac{1}{5}$

$\frac{1}{100}$
0.6
$\frac{7}{10}$
0.8

0.7
$\frac{2}{5}$
0.1
$\frac{9}{10}$

Finish
0.2
$\frac{3}{5}$
0.75
$\frac{1}{2}$

Teacher's Guide

See pages 104–5 of the *Teacher's Guide*. Explain the rules for each game and allow children to choose which to play. Encourage them to challenge themselves and practise what they have learnt in the unit.

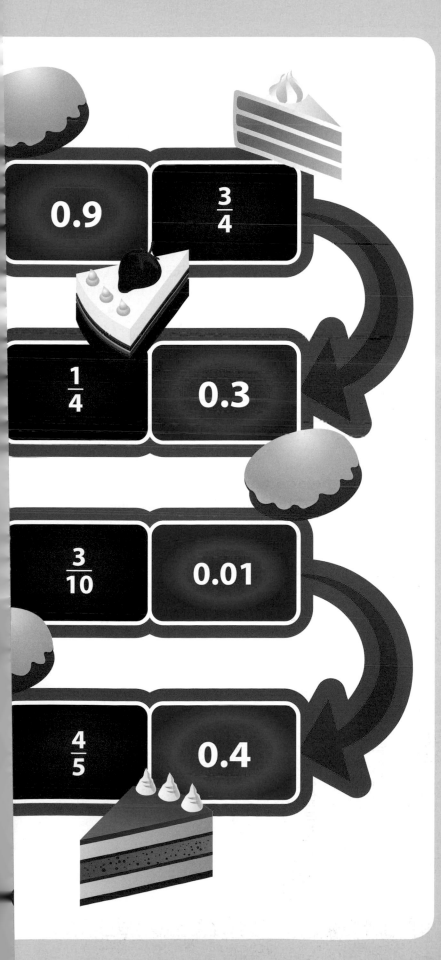

 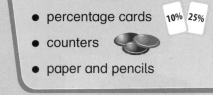
1 **Match up**

Match percentages with equivalent decimals and fractions to score points!

2 **Add up**

Total the fractions and decimals you land on to see who can get the highest score!

3 **Your game**

Design your own game. Explain the rules and play with a partner.

# Special numbers, operators and scaling

What do you notice about these bathroom tiles?

Look at the numbers on the football players' shirts. What have they got in common?

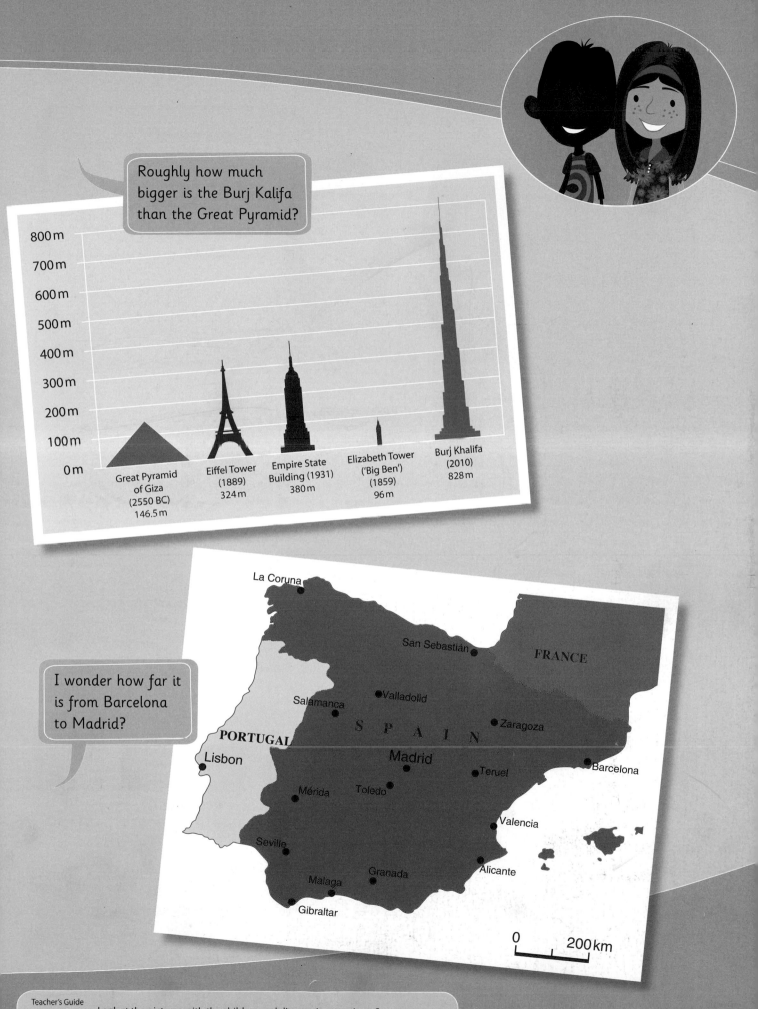

Roughly how much bigger is the Burj Kalifa than the Great Pyramid?

800 m
700 m
600 m
500 m
400 m
300 m
200 m
100 m
0 m

Great Pyramid of Giza (2550 BC) 146.5 m

Eiffel Tower (1889) 324 m

Empire State Building (1931) 380 m

Elizabeth Tower ('Big Ben') (1859) 96 m

Burj Khalifa (2010) 828 m

I wonder how far it is from Barcelona to Madrid?

La Coruna

San Sebastián

FRANCE

Salamanca

Valladolid

Zaragoza

S P A I N

PORTUGAL

Lisbon

Madrid

Teruel

Barcelona

Mérida

Toledo

Valencia

Seville

Granada

Alicante

Malaga

Gibraltar

0        200 km

Teacher's Guide

Look at the pictures with the children and discuss the questions. See pages 108–9 of the *Teacher's Guide* for key ideas to draw out.

95

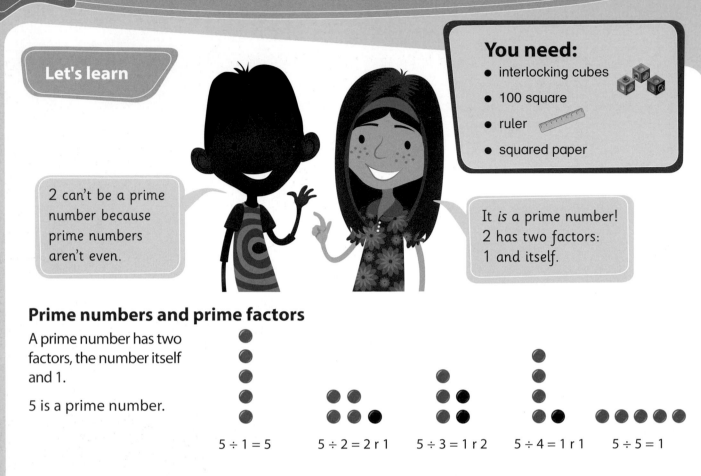

**Let's learn**

**You need:**
- interlocking cubes
- 100 square
- ruler
- squared paper

2 can't be a prime number because prime numbers aren't even.

It *is* a prime number! 2 has two factors: 1 and itself.

## Prime numbers and prime factors

A prime number has two factors, the number itself and 1.

5 is a prime number.

$5 \div 1 = 5$    $5 \div 2 = 2\,r\,1$    $5 \div 3 = 1\,r\,2$    $5 \div 4 = 1\,r\,1$    $5 \div 5 = 1$

A number that is not a prime is called a **composite number.**

Some factors are also prime numbers.

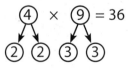

$4 \times 9 = 36$

$2 \times 2 \times 3 \times 3 = 36$

So the **prime factors** of 36 are 2, 2, 3 and 3.

What are the prime factors of 24?

## Square and cube numbers

A square number is a number that is multiplied by itself.

1 unit in length × 1 unit in width = 1 squared or $1^2$

What do you notice about the link between odd numbers and square numbers?

A cube number is a number multiplied by itself and then by itself again.

2 units in length × 2 units in width × 2 units in height = 2 cubed or $2^3$

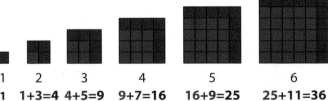

| Shape number | 1 | 2 | 3 | 4 | 5 | 6 |
|---|---|---|---|---|---|---|
| Number of small squares | 1 | 1+3=4 | 4+5=9 | 9+7=16 | 16+9=25 | 25+11=36 |

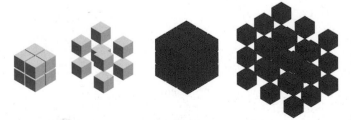

Teacher's Guide

Before working through the *Textbook*, study page 110 of the *Teacher's Guide* to see how the concepts should be introduced. Read and discuss the page with the children. Provide concrete resources to support exploration.

**1**

**Write.**

Write down the squares of all the numbers up to and including 12.

Write the multiplication statement for each one.

Now draw a square for each to prove that they are squares.

**2**

**Write.**

Write down the cubes of all the numbers up to and including 10.

Make cubes to show that you are correct. Which of your starting numbers are prime?

**3**

**Apply.**

Use a ruler to measure and draw these squares to check their areas:

a    If each side of a square is 12 cm, what is its area?

b    What would be the area of a square that has sides of 15 cm?

c    If a square has sides of 25 cm, what is its area?

**4**

**Investigate.**

When you add 2 prime numbers together, can you make a square number? Use a 100 square to help you investigate!

Can you make all the square numbers to 144 in this way?

Teacher's Guide    See page 111 of the *Teacher's Guide* for ideas of how to guide practice. Work through each step together as a class to develop children's conceptual understanding.

**97** ★

# Using fractions as operators for multiplication and division

**8b**

**Let's learn**

**You need:**
- place-value grids
- digit cards
- money
- ruler
- weighing scales

*I think 20p is 2% of £1.*

*2p is 2% of £1. 20p is 20% of £1 because it is 20 pence out of 100 pence.*

## Finding percentages

The grid represents 100% or £1.

£1 = 100p, so 1% of £1 = 1p and 10% of £1 = 10p.

How many other percentages of £1 can you find?

Can you find some more percentages of £26?

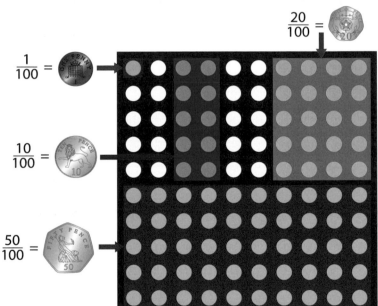

$\frac{1}{100} =$

$\frac{10}{100} =$

$\frac{50}{100} =$

$\frac{20}{100} =$

## Decimal equivalences

We know that $\frac{1}{10}$ is equivalent to 0.1 and also 10%, so 0.1 must be equivalent to 10%.

$\frac{1}{2}$ is equivalent to 0.5 and 50%.

Use the grid to work out what decimal is equivalent to $\frac{1}{5}$ and 20%.

**Find 26% of £12:**

Find 1% first, divide £12 by 100

| 10 | 1 | . | $\frac{1}{10}$ | $\frac{1}{100}$ |
|---|---|---|---|---|
| 1 | 2 | | | |
| | 1 | . | 2 | |

Then multiply by 26:

$0.12 \times 20 = 2.4$

$0.12 \times 6 = 0.72$

$2.4 + 0.72 = £3.12$

Teacher's Guide

Before working through the *Textbook*, study page 112 of the *Teacher's Guide* to see how the concepts should be introduced. Read and discuss the page with the children. Provide concrete resources to support exploration.

**1**

### Calculate.

Find the percentages of these amounts:

a     10% of £30        d     75% of £20        g     35% of £70

b     15% of £40        e     30% of £80        h     20% of £12.50

c     25% of £60        f     45% of £90

**2**

### Calculate.

Find the fractions and decimals of these amounts:

a     $\frac{1}{2}$ of £48        d     $\frac{2}{5}$ of £60        g     $\frac{3}{8}$ of £32

b     0.25 of £12        e     0.75 of £120        h     0.01 of £97

c     0.2 of £35        f     $\frac{1}{8}$ of £64

**3**

### Solve.

Find the percentages of these amounts by finding 1% or 10% first:

a     12% of 6 kg                 c     58% of 2750 g

b     30% of 150 cm             d     45% of 3200 ml

Now measure these new amounts using rulers, scales and measuring cylinders.

**4**

### Think.

Sophie's friend offered her 15% of £50, $\frac{1}{5}$ of £30 or 0.25 of £20.
Which offer should Sophie take
if she wants the most money?

> Think about what you must do to compare the percentages, fractions and decimals.

Explain why you made this decision.

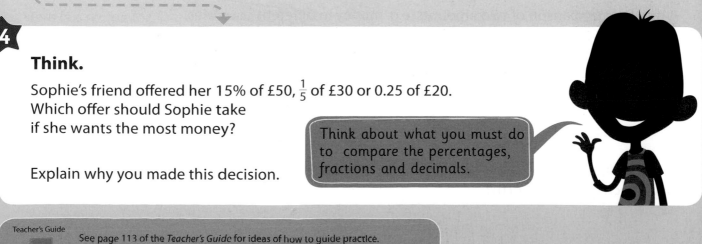

Teacher's Guide    See page 113 of the *Teacher's Guide* for ideas of how to guide practice. Work through each step together as a class to develop children's conceptual understanding.

# Higher and higher

Let's play

Start

2

5

8

10

12

3

4

6

1

Finish

9

1

Teacher's Guide

See pages 116–17 of the *Teacher's Guide*. Explain the rules for each game and allow children to choose which to play. Encourage them to challenge themselves and practise what they have learnt in the unit.

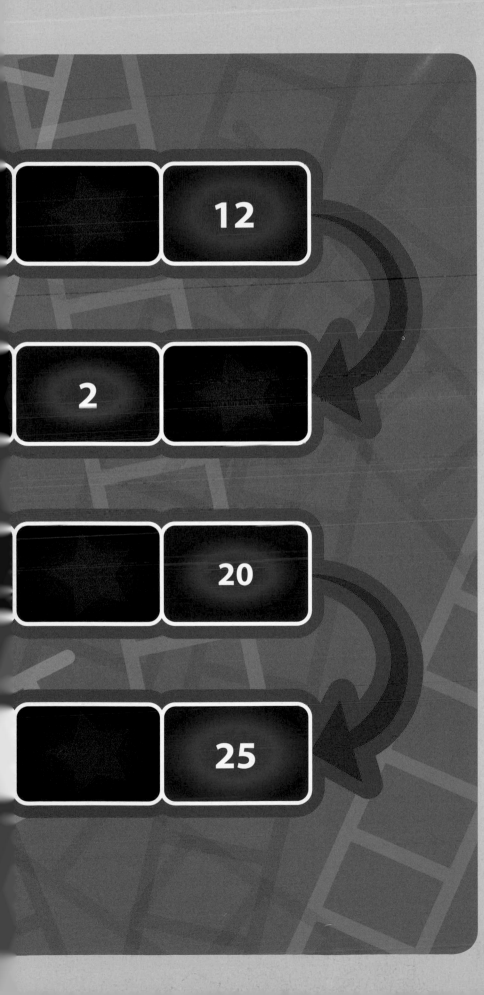

12

2

20

25

**1** **Going up!**
Scale up the numbers and see who can score the highest total.

**2** **Going down!**
Scale down the numbers and see who can score the lowest total.

**3** **Your game**
Design your own game. Explain the rules and play with a partner.

# And finally ...

Let's review

**1**

I think prime numbers are always odd numbers.

I think square numbers always have an odd number of factors.

Is this always, sometimes or never true?
Explain why.
Write down some prime numbers to prove your thinking.

Is this always, sometimes or never true?
Explain why.
Write down some square numbers and their factors to prove your thinking.

**2**

Find these:

**a** 10% of £35

**b** $\frac{2}{5}$ of 6 kg

**c** 0.1 of 50 m

**d** $\frac{7}{10}$ of 250 l

Now find these fractions of time:

**i** $\frac{5}{12}$ of 1 hour

**j** 0.3 of 3 hours

**k** 0.75 of 5 hours

**l** $\frac{1}{3}$ of 21 days

**e** 24% of £200

**f** 15% of 75 kg

**g** 0.8 of 120 cm

**h** $\frac{3}{5}$ of £68

**m** 0.9 of 40 days

**n** 70% of a millennium

**o** 31% of a century

**p** $\frac{7}{10}$ of a minute

Teacher's Guide

See pages 118–19 of the *Teacher's Guide* for guidance on running each task. Observe children to identify those who have mastered concepts and those who require further consolidation.

**3**

**a** Draw a diagram to show that 25 has been scaled up 6 times.
Now draw another diagram to show the 25 has been scaled up by another amount …
and another …
and another …
and another!

**b** Draw a diagram to show a number has been made $\frac{1}{6}$ of the size.
Now draw another …
and another …
and another!

**c** Choose your own scale factor to scale up these numbers:
15, 45, 110, 750

**d** Decide on a scale factor to scale your numbers down by, e.g. $\frac{1}{3}$ or $\frac{1}{8}$.

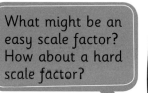
What might be an easy scale factor? How about a hard scale factor?

# Did you know?

The largest prime number so far was found in 2013. It has 17 425 170 digits!

Our number system goes on to infinity. So mathematicians will be working to find the highest one forever!

```
56528 42717 90118 81855 20030 27876 63574 14244 48193 15465 81365 97545 26948 00024 72273 60759 69740
       10929 34353 33570 60205 44225 60727 55269 17620 69944 62858 63033 62376 58179 19922 9468
    46 32510 66116 02434 73929 52411 31428 23141 78142 01482 91477 44880 96088 28685 4876
    58 15305 35668 98368 07610 51991 79393 46318 22097 57424 53436 75856 13835 07837 8637
    29 94727 94609 36250 96255 12982 47823 57845 73105 57062 43933 60651 78915 81461 0176
    29 22990 67778 23446 53107 06385 85039 30393 85893 26581 79631 90579 63315 64359 0231
    47 42197 45959 08275 10898 84404 80606 70193 86329 31642 78436 44788 17775 71884 9407
    73 52765 91870 23054 77013 05241 66161 60839 46609 79366 60668 79638 53287 61518 4695
    26 12601 80742 63656 97274 31587 03580 08245 79121 64478 19612 94753 86831 22108 0508
    37 32083 51546 99724 14328 75483 60267 01252 39211 50534 45547 86819 54002 72761 5030
    69 46354 22515 81794 13456 25887 66249 80466 78916 12504 76452 11068 96276 96248 7176
   39 66019 93268 56170 39151 40507 95670 37145 85041 16885 29190 90591 87891 36597 66692 9122
  23 31297 55383 28652 93583 70110 97156 72467 58931 16151 74261 22070 25113 98978 42650 95254 0458
 529 76489 60240 04693 08485 71952 95614 18634 97161 49672 86233 35669 04247 89091 09756 85949 06446
70521 41267 85386 53311 85388 39079 85894 79704 94333 70596 72631 55717 50505 16605 68699 40880 03709
28402 14590 64336 67768 20042 46699 97729 67654 21060 08604 47245 00465 50527 58905 06830 60816 60637
01246 71284 88211 18118 47095 29275 45572 66969 18551 99270 77698 82733 55419 65784 80744 65839 25018
92801 23154 37943 94215 41913 99430 28055 79844 36172 53975 25036 98055 50157 74649 17207 79507 81828
87613 49857 92332 56900 54829 75331 60505 98738 82543 48788 21594 82147 06484 59255 92146 87264 75495
50143 72517 87269 13705 67991 42555 70950 83644 27594 29900 69222 95855 84722 79575 83593 26534 13595
22871 77391 97658 39814 72454 62274 36478 67286 86969 02392 77010 10652 87414 44661 74533 69353 66418
24333 36303 13454 70794 15940 35078 31689 59979 53652 34316 10950 40619 14198 58318 44848 80638 66361
46872 70400 09940 80827 24499 78466 41768 26418 33446 43866 15766 06503 12157 83361 14577 54314 17409
75167 40732 07146 54200 03824 77441 51581 95134 49665 72857 32808 28389 91574 04950 40476 69129 91980
47608 99904 66867 69906 81819 50063 49980 54417 85656 75123 81819 72802 35128 70819 76463 39705 74179
21168 88223 19193 42371 82495 43505 80242 61207 19350 18220 93079 40661 18331 99476 32458 10337 14035
88554 57665 73324 91328 04466 20029 94728 19508 44589 46866 97566 31240 36933 91283 00764 14879 40175
57452 21963 15783 38285 80226 98377 53282 50683 18950 03231 97893 33874 36758 18090 43438 97931 22181
```

# 2-D and 3-D shapes

I wonder what happens to shapes when they are reflected?

Are there translations in this patterned quilt?

I wonder what different faces and angles this beautiful diamond has?

I wonder why these roofs have different angles?

Where else can you see reflex angles?

Teacher's Guide

Look at the pictures with the children and discuss the questions.
See pages 120–1 of the *Teacher's Guide* for key ideas to draw out.

**107** ⭐

Let's learn

The question says draw a reflex angle of 310° but my protractor only measures up to 180°. It's impossible!

I disagree. It's possible because the angles around a point total 360°. Can you work out how to do it now?

## Drawing and measuring reflex angles

A protractor can only measure angles up to 180° but reflex angles are greater than 180°. You can still use a protractor to measure and draw accurate reflex angles.

You can work out the measurement of the smaller angle and then take it away from 360 (a full circle).

Or you can measure how much greater than 180° (a straight line) the angle is and add that measurement to 180°.

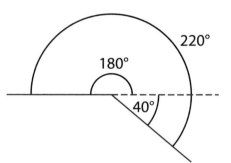

## Calculating angles on a straight line

A straight line angle is 180°. You can use this fact to find missing angles.

You can write the missing angle as $x = 180° - 43°$, so $x = 137°$.

Teacher's Guide

Before working through the *Textbook*, study page 126 of the *Teacher's Guide* to see how the concepts should be introduced. Read and discuss the page with the children. Provide concrete resources to support exploration.

## 1

**Answer these.**

Calculate these reflex angles.

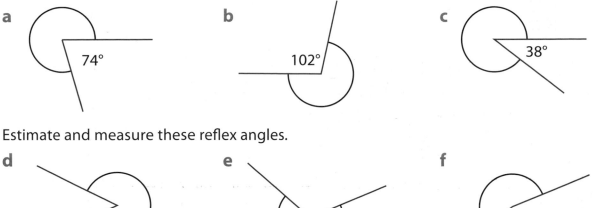

a  74°

b  102°

c  38°

Estimate and measure these reflex angles.

d

e

f

## 2

**Draw.**

Choose 2 angles from the table.

a  Draw a sketch of them around a point and calculate the missing reflex angles.

b  Use a protractor to draw the angles accurately.

| 34° | 28° | 67° | 98° |
| 19° | 42° | 71° | 53° |

## 3

**Apply.**

Find 4 examples of reflex angles in your classroom or playground. Estimate, measure and draw the angles.

Review the accuracy of your estimates.

## 4

**Think.**

Copy the table. Draw a polygon that matches the properties described. Label the acute angles A, obtuse angles O and reflex angles R.

| Property | No equal sides | One pair of equal sides | Two pairs of equal sides |
|---|---|---|---|
| No parallel sides | | | |
| One pair of parallel sides | | | |
| Two pairs of parallel sides | | | |

Can you see any patterns in the angles?

Explain your thinking to a friend.

Teacher's Guide

See page 127 of the *Teacher's Guide* for ideas of how to guide practice. Work through each step together as a class to develop children's conceptual understanding.

**113**

# 3-D shapes challenge

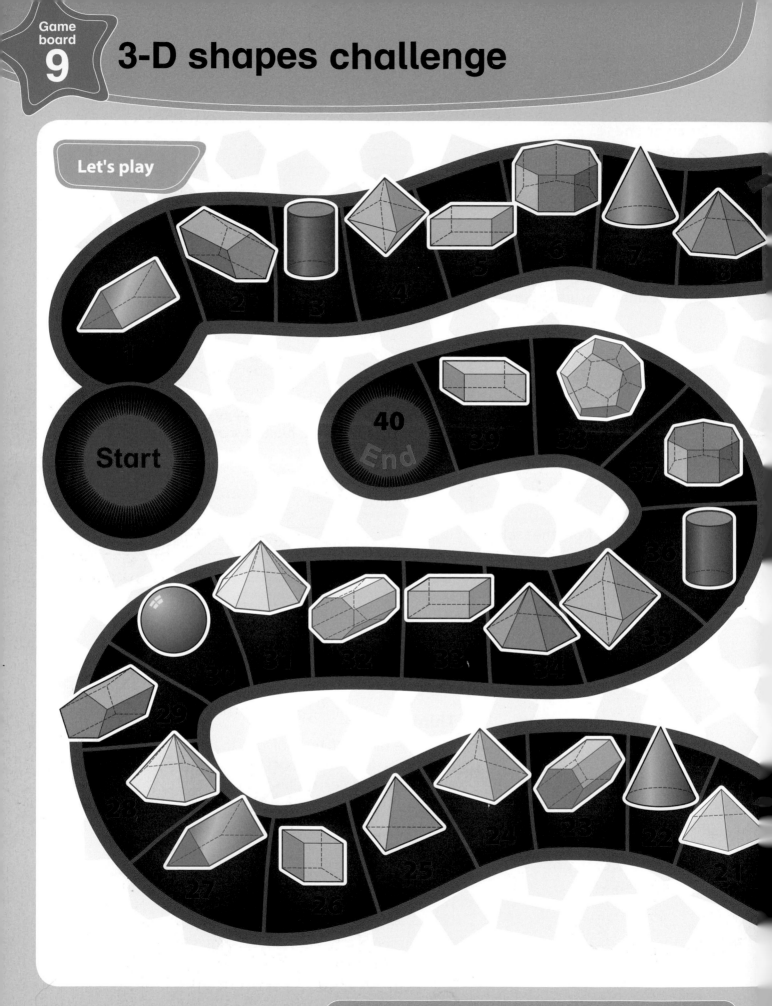

Let's play

Start

40 End

Teacher's Guide

See pages 128–9 of the *Teacher's Guide*. Explain the rules for each game and allow children to choose which to play. Encourage them to challenge themselves and practise what they have learnt in the unit.

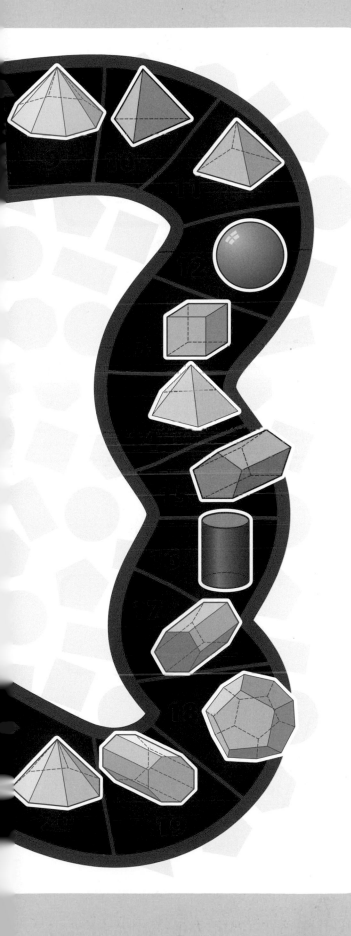

## You need:

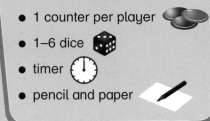

- 1 counter per player
- 1–6 dice
- timer
- pencil and paper

### ⭐1 Edge to the finish!

Score points that match the number of edges of each 3-D shape you land on.

Who will be the player with the highest score?

### ⭐2 Faces and vertices!

Race to the end of the track by scoring points according to the properties of the shape you land on.

Will you be the player with the highest score?

### ⭐3 Your game

Design your own game. Explain the rules and play with a partner.

# And finally ...

**1**

Follow these instructions:

**You need:**
- cm-squared paper
- protractor

- Draw a grid with $x$- and $y$-axes labelled 1–10.
- Draw a quadrilateral that includes a reflex angle and has no coordinate greater than 5.
- Write down the coordinates of your quadrilateral.
- Draw the mirror line $x = 5$ on your grid.
- Reflect your quadrilateral in the mirror line.
- Write down the coordinates of the reflected shape.
- Translate your original quadrilateral 2 squares left and 5 squares up.
- Write down the coordinates of the new position.
- Copy the coordinates of your original quadrilateral. Give them to your partner to complete the same operations.
- Check your answers with your partner's.
- Estimate the reflex angle in each other's quadrilateral.
- Use a protractor to measure the actual size of the angle.

**2**

**You need:**
- protractor
- ruler

**a**    Calculate the missing angles.

**b**    Use a protractor to make up your own set of missing angle problems. Make sure that you draw the angles accurately.

Teacher's Guide

See pages 130–1 of the *Teacher's Guide* for guidance on running each task. Observe children to identify those who have mastered concepts and those who require further consolidation.

**3**

Copy the table below and draw or place real shapes into it.
Are there any shapes that you cannot fit into the table?
Can you see any patterns?

|  | No triangular faces | One triangular face | More than one triangular face |
|---|---|---|---|
| Three edges at each vertex |  |  |  |
| More than three edges at one or more vertices |  |  |  |

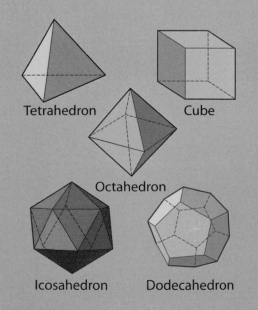

# Did you know?

3-D shapes where each face is the same regular polygon and where the same number of polygons meet at each vertex are called Platonic solids.

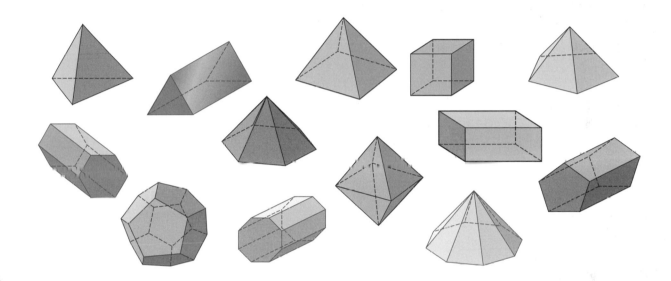

Tetrahedron

Cube

Octahedron

Icosahedron     Dodecahedron

There are only five Platonic solids. They are called Platonic solids after Plato, a Greek philosopher who lived over 2000 years ago and was interested in geometry.

| | | | DEBIT (£) | CREDIT (£) | BALANCE (£) |
|---|---|---|---|---|---|
| | **SHEET 19 ACCOUNT NO 82184669** | | | | |
| 18 JUN | SUNDRIES | 200303 | | 587.50 | 6480.00 |
| 19 JUN | | 100529 | 2350.00 | | 4130.00 |
| 19 JUN | | 100527 | 470.00 | | 3660.00 |
| 19 JUN | | 100528 | 117.50 | | 3542.50 |
| 20 JUN | | 100530 | 6000.00 | | −2457.5 |
| 20 JUN | WAGES | | | 2000.00 | −457.50 |
| 21 JUN | SUNDRIES | 200304 | 470.00 | | −927.5 |
| 21 JUN | INTEREST | | | 70.00 | −857.50 |
| 23 JUN | SUNDRIES | 200305 | | 352.50 | −505.00 |
| 24 JUN | | 100531 | 25.00 | | −530.00 |

Can you see any negative numbers on this bank statement?

I wonder what fraction of our diet should be made up of fruit and vegetables?

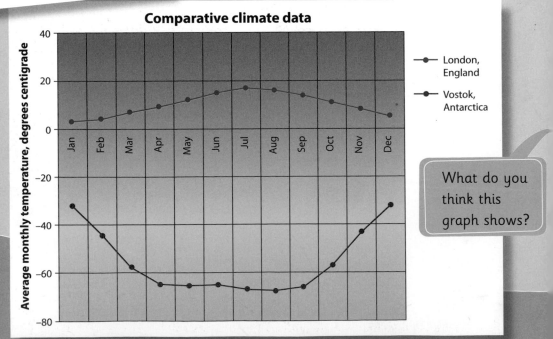

**Comparative climate data**

Average monthly temperature, degrees centigrade

London, England

Vostok, Antarctica

What do you think this graph shows?

What time does the last bus from Northampton arrive in Little Harrowden?

**Bus timetable**

| Northampton | 0750 | 0850 | 0950 | 1050 | 1150 | 1250 | 1350 | 1450 | 1550 |
|---|---|---|---|---|---|---|---|---|---|
| **Kingsley Road** | 0756 | 0856 | 0956 | 1056 | 1156 | 1256 | 1356 | 1456 | 1556 |
| Kingsley | 0759 | 0859 | 0959 | 1059 | 1159 | 1259 | 1359 | 1459 | 1559 |
| **Lumbertubs** | 0809 | 0909 | 1009 | 1109 | 1209 | 1309 | 1409 | 1509 | 1609 |
| Moulton Road | 0812 | 0912 | 1012 | 1112 | 1212 | 1312 | 1412 | 1512 | 1612 |
| **Moulton** | 0815 | 0915 | 1015 | 1115 | 1215 | 1315 | 1415 | 1515 | 1615 |
| Overstone Road | | | 1024 | | 1224 | | 1424 | | 1624 |
| **Overstone** | | | 1028 | | 1228 | | 1428 | | 1628 |
| Sywell | | | 1032 | | 1232 | | 1432 | | 1632 |
| **Mears Ashby** | | | 1037 | | 1237 | | 1437 | | 1637 |
| Little Harrowden | | | 1048 | | 1248 | | 1448 | | 1648 |

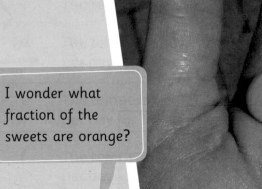

I wonder what fraction of the sweets are orange?

Let's review

**1**

I think that 1.04 kilogram is the same as 1 kilogram 4 grams and also 14 grams.

**You need:**
- place-value grids
- digit cards

Explain the mistake Theo has made and what 1.04 kg actually is equivalent to.

Now write down and explain to a partner what these masses are in kilograms and grams and then in grams.

a    5.25 kg

c    8.1 kg

e    2.2 kg

b    7.009 kg

d    10.075 kg

f    4.25 kg

Write down these volumes in litres.

g    $\frac{2500}{1000}$ ml

i    $\frac{1200}{1000}$ ml

k    $\frac{6400}{1000}$ ml

h    $\frac{6245}{1000}$ ml

j    $\frac{7050}{1000}$ ml

l    $\frac{3125}{1000}$ ml

**2**

Round these numbers to the nearest tenth, one and thousand.

a    4352.65

d    835 607.81

b    6984.19

e    174 365.12

c    27 241.57

f    234.736

**You need:**
- place-value grids
- digit cards

Now order the amounts you have rounded to the nearest thousand, from the lowest number to the highest.

Make up some of your own numbers to round to the nearest tenth, one and thousand.

Teacher's Guide

See pages 142–3 of the *Teacher's Guide* for guidance on running each task. Observe children to identify those who have mastered concepts and those who require further consolidation.

**3** Write these numbers using numerals.

**a**     One million three hundred and forty six thousand three hundred and two

**b**     One million and twenty one thousand three hundred and twenty

**c**     One million eight thousand seven hundred and seventy two

Write these numbers in words.

**d**     1 345 104

**e**     1 207 246

**f**     1 051 098

Now solve these problems.

**g**     The temperature was −60°C during the night. It had gone up by 10 degrees by lunchtime. What was the temperature at lunchtime?

**h**     It was 80°C one afternoon. The temperature had gone down by 14 degrees by midnight. What was the temperature at midnight?

**i**     The temperature was 12°C at 11:15 a.m. It had risen 15 degrees since 3 a.m. What was the temperature at 3 a.m.?

# Did you know?

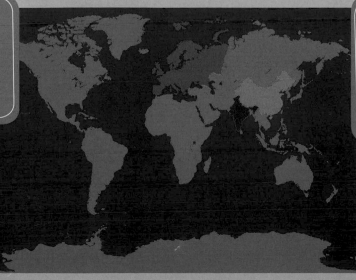

It's thought that negative numbers were first introduced in 200 BCE by the Chinese. They used them to show how much people owed other people.

Negative numbers appeared in India around 620 CE for the same reason. In Europe, most mathematicians didn't think that negative existed!

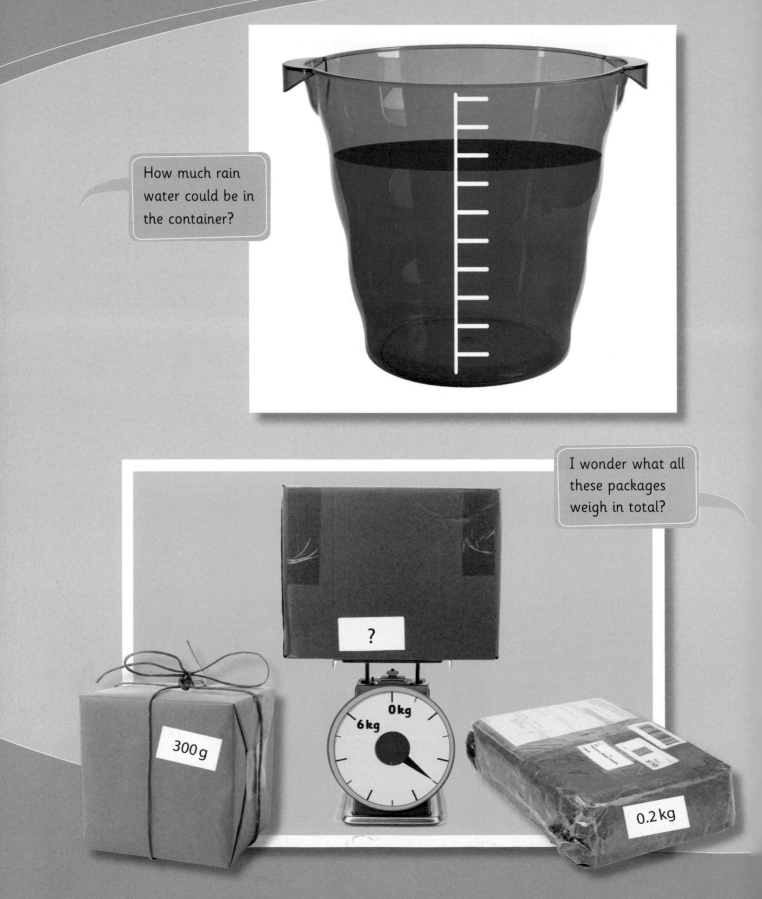

I wonder how you could show the same information in grams?

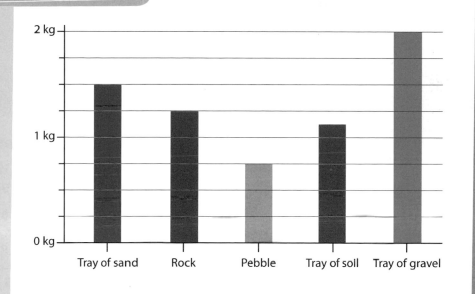

2 kg
1 kg
0 kg

Tray of sand    Rock    Pebble    Tray of soil    Tray of gravel

I have eaten more than you because I've had 2 slices!

Teacher's Guide    Look at the pictures with the children and discuss the questions. See pages 144–5 of the *Teacher's Guide* for key ideas to draw out.

131

# A moley mass!

**Let's play**

| 750 g Start | 0.25 kg | 135 g | 1300 g | 500 g | 0.142 kg |
|---|---|---|---|---|---|

| Miss a turn | 639 g | 0.25 kg | 255 g | 1450 g | 0.125 kg |
|---|---|---|---|---|---|

100 g

| Roll again | 600 g | 0.65 kg | $\frac{1}{2}$ kg | 700 g | 0.25 kg |
|---|---|---|---|---|---|

**?** Finish | 0.8 kg | 0.2 kg | 100 g

Teacher's Guide

See pages 150–1 of the *Teacher's Guide*. Explain the rules for each game and allow children to choose which to play. Encourage them to challenge themselves and practise what they have learnt in the unit.

| 0 g | 1450 g | 0.12 kg | Roll again |
| | | | $\frac{1}{2}$ kg |
| 5 g | 2180 g | 0.42 kg | Drop 0.1 kg |
| | 1000 g | 0.68 kg | Drop 1250 g |
| | | | 1.2 kg |
| 5 g | 1.5 kg | 75 g | Miss a turn |

## You need:

- counters
- 1–6 dice
- calculator

### 1 Mole marathon

Collect the soil along the way and add it to the mass already in your cart. The winner finishes the game with the most soil!

### 2 Tunnel troubles

This time you must subtract 0.75 kg of soil when you roll a 5 and subtract 825 g of soil when you roll a 6.

### 3 Your game

Design your own game. Explain the rules and play with a partner.

# And finally ...

Let's review

**1**

I wonder if I can use a mental method for each of these calculations?

| | |
|---|---|
| **a** 7599 + 1201 | **d** 11 722 − 9980 |
| **b** 1.75 kg + 1250 g | **e** 5265 g − 2 kg |
| **c** 3.125 litres + 999 ml | **f** 4349 ml − 2.165 litres |

What different methods could Theo use? Which method would be the most efficient?

**2**

| $\frac{5}{4}$ | $2\frac{1}{2}$ | $1\frac{4}{5}$ |
|---|---|---|
| $2\frac{6}{8}$ | $1\frac{1}{4}$ | $2\frac{3}{10}$ |

Look at the values in the grid. Think about the addition calculations you can make to find totals that sit in the shaded part of this number line.

1    2    3    4    5

Write a subtraction calculation using your own numbers where the difference will also fit in the shaded part of the number line.

Teacher's Guide

See pages 152–3 of the *Teacher's Guide* for guidance on running each task.
Observe children to identify those who have mastered concepts and those who require further consolidation.

**3**

Rain water was collected over a week in 2 different areas of the school.
Container A was placed in the playground and Container B by the nature area. This table shows the rain water collected.

|  | Monday | Tuesday | Wednesday | Thursday | Friday |
|---|---|---|---|---|---|
| **Container A** | 0.125 litres | 0.4 litres | 0.575 litres | 0.75 litres | 0.925 litres |
| **Container B** | 0.345 litres | 0.48 litres | 0.62 litres | 0.83 litres | 0.975 litres |

Is the difference between the water collected on Monday and Friday greater in Container A or in Container B?

## Did you know?

On 15th February 1971, the UK introduced the decimal currency that is still used today. 99% of businesses changed to the new currency in just 6 weeks!
The metric system makes in very easy to convert between units of measurement using place value, but some imperial measurements are still used in the UK (pints, feet, inches, miles), and conversion between these units is trickier!

Before 1971 the UK used coins called a half penny, penny, threepence, sixpence, shilling and some others too.

# Exploring fractions, decimals and percentages

I wonder what these volumes would look like as litres?

Special offer!
3 for the price of 2

White mushrooms

Mass: 200 g

Price: £1.00 per 100 g

White grapes

Mass: 220 g

Price: £1.20 per 100 g

Apples

Mass: 475 g

Price: 60p per 100 g

How much would it cost altogether to buy the mushrooms, grapes and apples?

If I shared my sweets between myself and a friend, I wonder what different fractions I could make?

15% off Sunhats

35% off T-shirts

Which item has been reduced in price the most?

20% off Rollerblades

10% off Sunglasses

Kids Clothes

WE'RE HIRING

50% OFF

Teacher's Guide

Look at the pictures with the children and discuss the questions.
See pages 154–5 of the *Teacher's Guide* for key ideas to draw out.

141

**Let's learn**

I don't think $\frac{2}{3}$ and $\frac{10}{15}$ can be equivalent fractions, because their denominators are different.

Yes, they can! They have the same value, even though they look different.

## Comparing and ordering fractions

Look at the fraction wall.
Compare $\frac{2}{3}$ and $\frac{10}{15}$. Are they equivalent?

Make a list of other equivalent fractions that you can see on the fraction wall.

One whole

Look at the clocks.
What fractions are shaded?

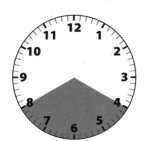

## Multiplying fractions by whole numbers

Look at the pattern when the numbers are multiplied.

What do you notice about the fractions?

When you multiply you find a fraction of the whole number.
$\frac{1}{2} \times 2$ is the same as $\frac{1}{2}$ of 2, which is 1.

What is $\frac{1}{3} \times 6$? $\frac{1}{5} \times 15$?

$$4 \times 2 = 8$$
$$3 \times 2 = 6$$
$$2 \times 2 = 4$$
$$1 \times 2 = 2$$
$$\frac{1}{2} \times 2 = 1$$
$$\frac{1}{4} \times 2 = \frac{1}{2}$$
$$\frac{1}{8} \times 2 = \frac{1}{4}$$

Teacher's Guide

Before working through the *Textbook*, study page 156 of the *Teacher's Guide* to see how the concepts should be introduced. Read and discuss the page with the children. Provide concrete resources to support exploration.

**1**

**Compare.**

$$\frac{1}{2} \quad \frac{1}{4} \quad \frac{3}{4} \quad \frac{1}{8} \quad \frac{3}{8} \quad \frac{7}{8}$$

Choose pairs of fractions and compare them using the symbols > and <. Do this 8 times.

Do the same again for these fractions.

$$\frac{1}{3} \quad \frac{2}{3} \quad \frac{3}{9} \quad \frac{7}{9} \quad \frac{8}{15} \quad \frac{11}{15}$$

Now order the fractions. Use your fraction strips to help you.

**2**

**Answer these.**

Multiply these fractions and whole numbers together.

a   $\frac{1}{2} \times 8$

c   $\frac{1}{10} \times 40$

e   $\frac{1}{8} \times 48$

g   $\frac{1}{5} \times 90$

b   $\frac{1}{4} \times 20$

d   $\frac{1}{6} \times 24$

f   $\frac{1}{3} \times 54$

h   $\frac{1}{12} \times 168$

Explain to a partner how you worked out your answers.

**3**

**Investigate.**

Multiply the fraction and the length. Draw your answers accurately with a ruler.

a   $\frac{1}{2} \times 12 \, cm$

e   $\frac{1}{12} \times 156 \, cm$

b   $\frac{1}{4} \times 28 \, cm$

f   $\frac{1}{5} \times 12.5 \, cm$

c   $\frac{1}{6} \times 42 \, cm$

g   $\frac{1}{10} \times 1.2 \, m$

d   $\frac{1}{8} \times 72 \, cm$

h   $\frac{1}{20} \times 2.8 \, m$

**4**

**Think.**

Illustrate your answers using diagrams.

$$\frac{1}{4} \times 2 = \frac{1}{2}$$

Use doubling and halving to make up other number statements from this one.

Teacher's Guide

See page 157 of the *Teacher's Guide* for ideas of how to guide practice. Work through each step together as a class to develop children's conceptual understanding.

**143**

# Working with decimals

**Let's learn**

I have a quick way of multiplying by 10, 100 and 1000. You just add zeros. 1 for 10, 2 for 100 and 3 for 1000.

That doesn't always work. If you multiply 5.1 by 10 using your way you will get 5.10, which is the same number!

**You need:**
- place-value grids
- digit cards 1 3 5
- coloured counters
- ruler

## Multiplying and dividing decimals by powers of 10

| | 10000 | 1000 | 100 | 10 | 1 | . | 10th | 100th | 1000th |
|---|---|---|---|---|---|---|---|---|---|
| | | | 3 | 6 | 5 | . | 7 | | |
| 365.7 × 100 | 3 | 6 | 5 | 7 | 0 | | | | |
| 365.7 ÷ 10 | | | | 3 | 6 | | 5 | 7 | |

Look at the place-value grid above.

365.7 × 100: each digit moves two places to the left. It becomes 100 times larger.

365.7 ÷ 10: each digit moves one place to the right. It becomes ten times smaller.

## Decimal numbers as fractions

| | | | | | | | | |
|---|---|---|---|---|---|---|---|---|
| 0.001 | 0.002 | 0.003 | 0.004 | 0.005 | 0.006 | 0.007 | 0.008 | 0.009 |
| 0.01 | 0.02 | 0.03 | 0.04 | 0.05 | 0.06 | 0.07 | 0.08 | 0.09 |
| 0.1 | 0.2 | 0.3 | 0.4 | 0.5 | 0.6 | 0.7 | 0.8 | 0.9 |
| 1 | 2 | 3 | 4 | 5 | 6 | 7 | 8 | 9 |
| 10 | 20 | 30 | 40 | 50 | 60 | 70 | 80 | 90 |
| 100 | 200 | 300 | 400 | 500 | 600 | 700 | 800 | 900 |
| 1000 | 2000 | 3000 | 4000 | 5000 | 6000 | 7000 | 8000 | 9000 |
| 10000 | 20000 | 30000 | 40000 | 50000 | 60000 | 70000 | 80000 | 90000 |
| 100000 | 200000 | 300000 | 400000 | 500000 | 600000 | 700000 | 800000 | 900000 |
| 1000000 | 2000000 | 3000000 | 4000000 | 5000000 | 6000000 | 7000000 | 8000000 | 9000000 |

Decimal numbers are fractions. They are less than one and have a decimal point in front of them.
Pick a number from the Gattegno chart above. Use it to make a 7-digit number with 3 decimal places. Write the decimal as a fraction.

0.001 is equivalent to $\frac{1}{1000}$

0.01 is equivalent to $\frac{1}{100}$

0.1 is equivalent to $\frac{1}{10}$

Teacher's Guide
Before working through the *Textbook*, study page 158 of the *Teacher's Guide* to see how the concepts should be introduced. Read and discuss the page with the children. Provide concrete resources to support exploration.

## 1

### Answer these.

Multiply these numbers by 10, 100 and 1000.

a 43.25

c 1568.28

b 312.3

d 5983.148

Explain what has happened to each digit.

Divide these numbers by 10, 100 and 1000.

e 6100

g 745

f 460

h 1456241

Explain what has happened to each digit.

## 2

### Write.

Write these decimals as proper fractions.

a 3.2

c 478. 68

e 12876.875

b 15.25

d 1793.125

f 142954.008

Reduce the fractions to their lowest terms.

## 3

### Apply.

Convert these measurements to decimals.

a $12\frac{1}{4}$ m

d $2375\frac{4}{5}$ km

b $5\frac{1}{2}$ cm

e $8\frac{1}{8}$ l

c $10\frac{3}{4}$ kg

f $37274\frac{7}{8}$ km

Now draw some lines that are a mixture of centimetres and millimetres in length. Label the length of each line using a fraction and a decimal representation.

## 4

### Think.

I am thinking of a number. I multiply it by 100, take away 1000 and halve it. Now I divide it by 10. My new number is 276.8.

What number did Theo start with?

Teacher's Guide

See page 159 of the Teacher's Guide for ideas of how to guide practice. Work through each step together as a class to develop children's conceptual understanding.

145

# Calculating and converting percentages

**Let's learn**

**You need:**
- strips of paper
- counters
- ruler

20% is always more than 10%. 20% of £200 is £40 and 10% is only £20. There, I've proved it!

Sometimes it is, your example is right, but not always. It depends on the amount you are finding a percentage of. 20% of £10 is £2, but 10% of £50 is £5, which is more than £2.

## Working out a percentage

| 100% | | | | | | | | | |
|---|---|---|---|---|---|---|---|---|---|
| 50% | | | | | 50% | | | | |
| 25% | | 25% | | 25% | | 25% | | | |
| 12.5% | 12.5% | 12.5% | 12.5% | 12.5% | 12.5% | 12.5% | 12.5% | | |
| 10% | 10% | 10% | 10% | 10% | 10% | 10% | 10% | 10% | 10% |

Percentages are amounts of a whole divided into hundredths. One per cent is equivalent to $\frac{1}{100}$. Percentages can also be shown as fractions or decimal fractions.

Percentages vary depending on the whole number:

10% of 50 is 5     10% of 100 is 10.

To work out a percentage find 10 per cent first.

Then multiply or divide to find other percentages.

How could you find 45% of £300?

## Percentages, fractions and decimals

One per cent is equivalent to $\frac{1}{100}$ and 0.1. Any percentage can be converted to a fraction and a decimal:

50% is equivalent to $\frac{50}{100}$ and 0.5

60% is equivalent to $\frac{60}{100}$ and 0.6

Teacher's Guide

Before working through the *Textbook*, study page 160 of the *Teacher's Guide* to see how the concepts should be introduced. Read and discuss the page with the children. Provide concrete resources to support exploration.

**1**

### Answer these.

a   20% of £60

c   75% of £88

e   57% of £365

b   5% of £12

d   60% of £268

f   94% of £428

Explain how you worked these out.

**2**

### Answer these.

Convert these percentages into fractions and decimals.

a   30%

c   54%

e   36%

b   48%

d   25%

f   75%

Explain how you worked these out.
Make sure you reduce the fractions to their lowest form.

**3**

### Apply.

Measure the length of the strip of paper your teacher has given you. This is 100%. Find these percentages of that length and draw them accurately.

a   10%

d   60%

b   20%

e   70%

c   30%

f   90%

Write the amounts if your strip represented 24 km.
What if it represented 32 kg?
What if it represented 16 l?

**4**

### Think.

I can find 17.5% by finding 10%, halving and adding.

Explain how Amy can do this.

Teacher's Guide   See page 161 of the *Teacher's Guide* for ideas of how to guide practice. Work through each step together as a class to develop children's conceptual understanding.

147

# Playing around with percentages!

Let's play

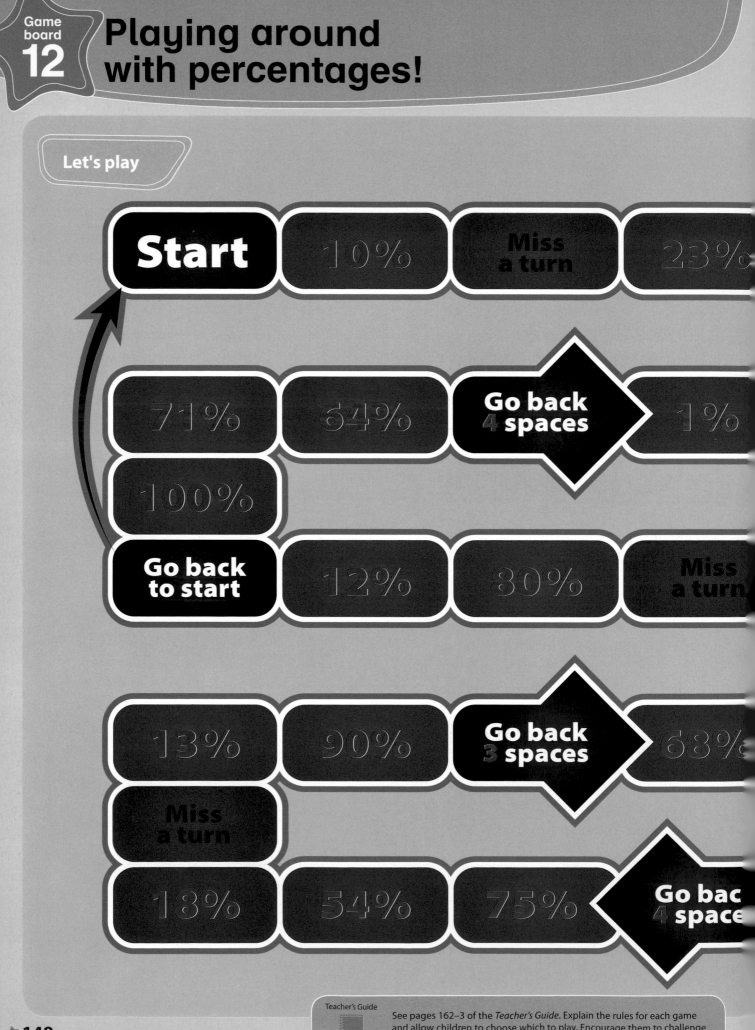

**Start** 10% **Miss a turn** 23%

71% 64% **Go back 4 spaces** 1%

100%

**Go back to start** 12% 80% **Miss a turn**

13% 90% **Go back 3 spaces** 68%

**Miss a turn**

18% 54% 75% **Go bac 4 space**

Teacher's Guide

See pages 162–3 of the *Teacher's Guide*. Explain the rules for each game and allow children to choose which to play. Encourage them to challenge themselves and practise what they have learnt in the unit.

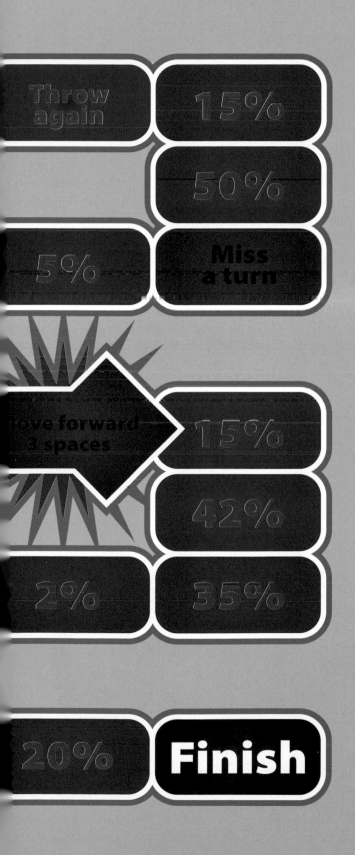

**You need:**

- 2-digit number cards
- counters
- 1–6 dice

### 1 Find the percentage

Find the percentages of different numbers to find your score. The winner is the player with the most points!

### 2 Decimal challenge

Move around the board, converting percentages to decimals. The highest or lowest score wins – you decide!

### 3 Your game

Design your own game. Explain the rules and play with a partner.

Board spaces: Throw again, 15%, 50%, 5%, Miss a turn, Move forward 3 spaces, 15%, 42%, 2%, 35%, 20%, **Finish**

**Let's review**

**1**

10% is equivalent to 0.1 and $\frac{1}{10}$.

Explain why Theo is correct.

Write down and explain to a partner what these percentages are as decimals and fractions.

| a | 5% | c | 75% | e | 60% |
| b | 25% | d | 20% | f | 85% |

Write 6 decimals of your choice. Convert them to fractions and percentages.

**2**

Order these fractions from lowest to highest.

**a** $\frac{1}{4}, \frac{1}{2}, \frac{1}{8}, \frac{1}{3}$

**c** $\frac{3}{4}, \frac{2}{5}, \frac{3}{10}, \frac{4}{5}$

**b** $\frac{1}{10}, \frac{1}{5}, \frac{1}{2}, \frac{1}{3}$

**d** $\frac{2}{3}, \frac{1}{6}, \frac{7}{12}, \frac{5}{6}$

Multiply all the fractions in **a** by 2 and then 5.
Multiply all the fractions in **b** by 6 and then 9.

Now convert your fractions to decimals and percentages.

Teacher's Guide

See pages 164–5 of the *Teacher's Guide* for guidance on running each task. Observe children to identify those who have mastered concepts and those who require further consolidation.

**3**

Measure the 6 strips of paper your teacher has given you.

Write down what their lengths would be if they were 10% of the length.

Now work out what they would if they were:

**a**    30% of the length

**b**    25% of the length

**c**    60% of the length

**d**    85% of the length

**You need:**
- strips of paper
- ruler

# Did you know?

We use percentages in everyday life - from discounts in sales to the nutrients on food packaging.

I know some surprising percentages. A jellyfish is 95% water! We throw away 33% of all the food in the world that is intended to be eaten.

95% water

I wonder what this mass is in pounds?

**78p**
**per cake**

How much would it cost me in total to buy 15 cupcakes?

Could you work out how many millilitres would be in 8 glasses of milk?

MILK

2.6 litres

568 ml = 1 pint

I wonder what the volume of this present is?

Teacher's Guide
Look at the pictures with the children and discuss the questions.
See pages 166–7 of the *Teacher's Guide* for key ideas to draw out.

153

**All about factors**

Let's learn

I can find the prime factors of 12. They are 1, 2 and 3.

1 isn't a prime factor! Prime factors are prime numbers. Prime numbers have two factors. 1 only has one.

**You need:**
- ruler

|    | 1  | 2  | 3  | 4  | 5  | 6  | 7  | 8  | 9   | 10  | 11  | 12  |
|----|----|----|----|----|----|----|----|----|-----|-----|-----|-----|
| 1  | 1  | 2  | 3  | 4  | 5  | 6  | 7  | 8  | 9   | 10  | 11  | 12  |
| 2  | 2  | 4  | 6  | 8  | 10 | 12 | 14 | 16 | 18  | 20  | 22  | 24  |
| 3  | 3  | 6  | 9  | 12 | 15 | 18 | 21 | 24 | 27  | 30  | 33  | 36  |
| 4  | 4  | 8  | 12 | 16 | 20 | 24 | 28 | 32 | 36  | 40  | 44  | 48  |
| 5  | 5  | 10 | 15 | 20 | 25 | 30 | 35 | 40 | 45  | 50  | 55  | 60  |
| 6  | 6  | 12 | 18 | 24 | 30 | 36 | 42 | 48 | 54  | 60  | 66  | 72  |
| 7  | 7  | 14 | 21 | 28 | 35 | 42 | 49 | 56 | 63  | 70  | 77  | 84  |
| 8  | 8  | 16 | 24 | 32 | 40 | 48 | 56 | 64 | 72  | 80  | 88  | 96  |
| 9  | 9  | 18 | 27 | 36 | 45 | 54 | 63 | 72 | 81  | 90  | 99  | 108 |
| 10 | 10 | 20 | 30 | 40 | 50 | 60 | 70 | 80 | 90  | 100 | 110 | 120 |
| 11 | 11 | 22 | 33 | 44 | 55 | 66 | 77 | 88 | 99  | 110 | 121 | 132 |
| 12 | 12 | 24 | 36 | 48 | 60 | 72 | 84 | 96 | 108 | 120 | 132 | 144 |

## Factors

Look at the factors of 24, 48 and 96 in the multiplication grid. Factors are the numbers you multiply together to get another number. These are called multiplicands and multipliers.

multiplier

$$6 \times 8 = 48$$

multiplicand     product

In division, divisors and quotients are factors of the dividend.

divisor

$$108 \div 12 = 9$$

dividend     quotient

## Prime factor trees

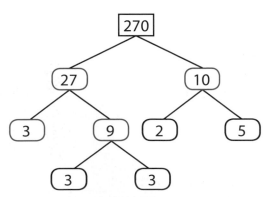

This is a prime factor tree. The number at the top is the multiple. The two numbers below (27 and 10) are the factor pairs.

This continues until there are only prime factors.

Teacher's Guide

Before working through the *Textbook*, study page 168 of the *Teacher's Guide* to see how the concepts should be introduced. Read and discuss the page with the children. Provide concrete resources to support exploration.

**1**

### Write.

Write 2 multiplication and 2 division statements to show the factors of these numbers.

a    12                c    125                e    2484

b    36                d    1350

Now circle all the factors.

**2**

### Draw.

Draw prime factor trees for these multiples.

a    84                c    150                e    500

b    144               d    280               f    372

**3**

### Investigate.

Use a ruler to draw lines that are the lengths of all the prime numbers to 20.

**4**

### Think.

What number is Theo thinking of?

> I am thinking of a number.
> It is an even number.
> It has an odd number of factors.
> It is less than 200.
> Its prime factors are 2, 2, 2, 2, 3, 3.

Make up some clues for a number for your partner to investigate. Can they find the number you are thinking of?

Teacher's Guide
See page 169 of the *Teacher's Guide* for ideas of how to guide practice. Work through each step together as a class to develop children's conceptual understanding.

155

Let's learn

**You need:**
- sets of digit cards
- counters
- squared paper
- sand
- scales
- plastic bags

When I multiply a number by 15 I use long multiplication.

It might be quicker to multiply the number by 10, halve it and add the 2 numbers together.

## Mental calculation

Use mental calculation when it is likely to be quicker than a written method.

Talk to your partner about the strategies below.

**× 15: × 10, halve and add**

| 246 × 10 = 2460 | 246 × 5 = 1230 |
|---|---|
| 246 × 15 = 3690 | |

**× 20: × 10 and double**

| 138 × 10 = 1380 | 138 × 10 = 1380 |
|---|---|
| 138 × 20 = 2760 | |

**× 4: double and double**

| 56 | 56 | 56 | 56 |
|---|---|---|---|
| 56 × 4 = 224 | | | |

**× 5: × 10 and halve**

| 284 × 10 = 2840 |
|---|
| 284 × 5 = 1420 |

## Scaling up and down

To multiply by scaling up you increase the size by a certain number of times. To divide by scaling down you find a fraction of the size.

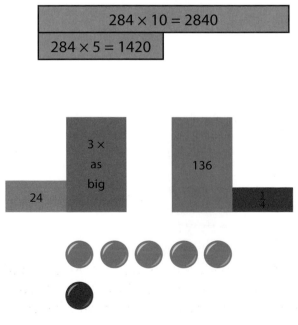

3 × as big

24

136

$\frac{1}{4}$

The purple counters represent 5 times the number of green counters.

If the green counter represents 125, what number is shown by the purple counters?

Teacher's Guide

Before working through the *Textbook*, study page 170 of the *Teacher's Guide* to see how the concepts should be introduced. Read and discuss the page with the children. Provide concrete resources to support exploration.

## 1

### Answer these.

Use mental calculation strategies for multiplication to answer these.

| | | | |
|---|---|---|---|
| **a** | 87 × 15 | **c** | 468 × 5 |
| **b** | 146 × 4 | **d** | 2354 × 20 |

Explain how you worked out each answer.

### Answer these.

Use mental calculation strategies for division to answer these.

| | | | |
|---|---|---|---|
| **e** | 90 ÷ 5 | **g** | 698 ÷ 20 |
| **f** | 248 ÷ 4 | **h** | 2480 ÷ 5 |

Explain how you worked out each answer.

## 2

### Answer these.

Draw bar models to solve these problems.

**a** Sam had 25 marbles. Ben had 5 times as many marbles. How many marbles did Ben have?

**b** Penny had 38 cherries. Suzi had 6 times as many. How many cherries did they have altogether?

**c** Nafisat had £10. Alfonso had a quarter of that amount. How much money did they have altogether?

**d** Bertie had a piece of string that was 2 metres in length. Moses had a piece an eighth of that length. How much more string did Bertie have?

> Now make up 4 of your own problems involving measures.

## 3

### Measure.

Measure out the following amounts of sand into plastic bags:

| | | | | | |
|---|---|---|---|---|---|
| **a** | 150 g | **c** | 90 g | **e** | 185 g |
| **b** | 325 g | **d** | 275 g | **f** | 235 g |

Draw a bar model diagram to show what each of these amounts would be scaled up by 6. Measure out the new amounts to compare with your original bags.

## 4

### Investigate.

Draw a bar. Label it as 36.

Draw a second bar underneath that is 3 times longer.

Find the value of the longer bar.

Now draw more bars and find their values. Make sure you scale up and scale down.

Teacher's Guide
See page 171 of the *Teacher's Guide* for ideas of how to guide practice. Work through each step together as a class to develop children's conceptual understanding.

157

# 4-digit and long multiplication

**Let's learn**

I had to multiply 145 and 23. So I multiplied 145 by 3 and then by 2 and then added the answers. My final answer was 725. My teacher said it was the wrong answer.

**You need:**
- counters
- digit cards  1 3 5
- money (coins)  5p 1p 10p

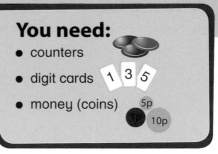

She was right. You multiplied 145 by 3 which is good. Then you multiplied by 2 when you should have multiplied by 20. 23 is 20 + 3.

## 4-digit multiplication

To multiply you can use arrays, the grid method or the written method. What is the same and different about these methods? Use the array to help compare them.

**3546 × 3**

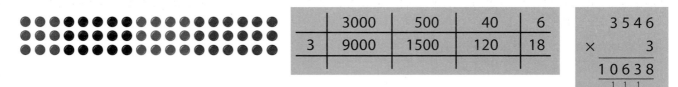

|   | 3000 | 500 | 40 | 6 |
|---|------|-----|----|----|
| 3 | 9000 | 1500 | 120 | 18 |

```
  3 5 4 6
×       3
---------
1 0 6 3 8
  1 1 1
```

9000 + 1500 + 120 + 18 = 10 638

## Long multiplication

In long multiplication you multiply by a multiplier that is more than a single digit. Sometimes 2 calculations can make it easier.

**567 × 24**

|    | 500   | 60   | 7   |
|----|-------|------|-----|
| 20 | 10000 | 1200 | 140 |
| 4  | 2000  | 240  | 28  |

```
  1 1 3 4 0
+   2 2 6 8
-----------
  1 3 6 0 8
        1
```

```
    5 6 7        5 6 7
×    2 0    ×       4
---------    ---------
1 1 3 4 0      2 2 6 8
    1 1            2 2
```

```
  1 1 3 4 0
+   2 2 6 8
-----------
  1 3 6 0 8
        1
```

What is the same and different about these methods of multiplication?

Teacher's Guide    Before working through the *Textbook*, study page 172 of the *Teacher's Guide* to see how the concepts should be introduced. Read and discuss the page with the children. Provide concrete resources to support exploration.

## 1

### Answer these.

Set these calculations out as arrays. Draw the grid method to find the answers.

**a**  4598 × 3              **c**  5378 × 7              **e**  8367 × 8

**b**  7254 × 6              **d**  3182 × 9              **f**  9875 × 6

Check your answers using the written method.

Answer these long multiplication calculations. Use the written method.

**g**  453 × 14             **i**  2874 × 23             **k**  4256 × 32

**h**  754 × 18             **j**  3985 × 27             **l**  5892 × 38

Check your answers using the grid method.

## 2

### Use long multiplication.

Make a 4-digit number using 4 digit cards. This is your multiplicand. Take 2 more cards and make a 2-digit number using 2 digit cards. This is your multiplier. Find the product. Use any method you wish.

Do this 5 times.

## 3

### Investigate.

Use £1 coins, 10p and 1p coins. Make an amount between £5 and £10. Scale your amount up 15 times. Use the grid method or the written method for long multiplication.

Now scale your amount up by 16 and then 24.

## 4

### Think.

I can answer 2456 × 8 in at least 4 different ways.

What 4 ways do you think Amy would do this? Demonstrate them.

Teacher's Guide

See page 173 of the *Teacher's Guide* for ideas of how to guide practice. Work through each step together as a class to develop children's conceptual understanding.

**159** ★

# 13d Division with remainders

**You need:**
- counters
- digit cards 1 3 5

## Let's learn

There are 125 children going on a school trip. They will travel in minibuses that each hold 20 children. I think 6 minibuses will be needed.

That's not quite right. 20 multiplied by 6 is 120. 125 children are going on the trip. You will have left 5 children behind! They will need 7 minibuses.

## Division

1995 ÷ 9. How many groups of 9 can you make from 1995?

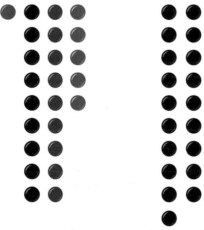
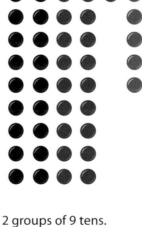

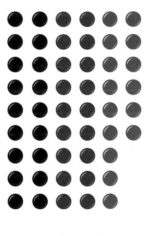

Exchange the thousand for hundreds.

2 groups of 9 hundreds. Exchange 1 left over for tens.

2 groups of 9 tens. Exchange 1 left over for ones.

1 group of 9 ones, with 6 left. The answer is 221 R 6.

The short method for this division is:

$$\begin{array}{r} 2\,2\,1\,R\,6 \\ 9\overline{)1^19^19^15} \end{array}$$

What is the same and what is different about these methods?

## Remainders

Remainders are important in division. They are usually shown as a number after R or as a fraction or decimal. In the example the remainder could be R6, $\frac{6}{9}$, $\frac{2}{3}$ or 0.6 as an approximate decimal.

Teacher's Guide

Before working through the *Textbook*, study page 174 of the *Teacher's Guide* to see how the concepts should be introduced. Read and discuss the page with the children. Provide concrete resources to support exploration.

**1**

### Answer these.

Write the remainders to these calculations as a fraction and a decimal.

**a**    $986 \div 8 = 123$ R 2      **c**    $298 \div 4 = 74$ R 2      **e**    $2589 \div 6 = 431$ R 3

**b**    $876 \div 5 = 175$ R 1      **d**    $1879 \div 10 = 187$ R 9

Answer these. Write any remainders as fractions.

**f**    $368 \div 8$      **h**    $345 \div 4$      **j**    $1287 \div 4$

**g**    $984 \div 3$      **i**    $897 \div 5$

**2**

### Use division.

Make a 4-digit number using 4 digit cards. This is your dividend. Take a 5th card as your divisor. This must be a number between 5 and 9. Find the quotient when you divide the dividend by the divisor. Write any remainders as fractions or decimals.

Do this 5 times.

**3**

### Investigate.

A box of 560 books arrived in the library. Sally was asked to put 9 books on each shelf in the children's section. How many shelves did she put books on?

Make up some problems like this for a friend to answer.

**4**

### Think.

> I know there will be no remainder for the calculation $2466 \div 9$ before I even answer it.

Theo is correct. How does he know this?

Teacher's Guide

See page 175 of the *Teacher's Guide* for ideas of how to guide practice. Work through each step together as a class to develop children's conceptual understanding.

**161**

# Mental maths!

Let's play

**Start**

× 15   ÷ 4   × 5   ☺

× 20   ☺   ÷ 2   ☺

× 15

☺   ÷ 20   × 5   × 5

× 20   ☺   ÷ 2   ☺

**Finish**

Teacher's Guide

See pages 176–7 of the *Teacher's Guide*. Explain the rules for each game and allow children to choose which to play. Encourage them to challenge themselves and practise what they have learnt in the unit.

**You need:**
- digit cards
- counters
- 1–6 dice

### 1 Pick more points
Start with 100 and multiply and divide. Who will have the most points when you reach the Finish?

### 2 Scaling race
Scale up and down and race to the Finish!

### 3 Your game
Design your own game. Explain the rules and play with a partner.

**163** ★

# And finally ...

**1**

I can multiply any number by 5 by multiplying it by 10 and halving.

Explain how he can do this.

I can multiply any number by 4 by doubling and doubling again.

Explain why this works.

And I can multiply using known facts.

Give 10 examples of multiplication statements that you know from 8 × 7 = 56.

**2**

This diagram shows that 48 has been made smaller by a quarter.

Now draw your own diagram to show that 48 has been scaled down by another amount.
And another …
And another …
And another!

48

12

Draw a diagram that shows 50 has been scaled up by 7.
Draw another diagram to show 50 has been scaled up by another amount.
And another …
And another …
And another!

Teacher's Guide

See pages 178–9 of the Teacher's Guide for guidance on running each task.
Observe children to identify those who have mastered concepts and those who require further consolidation.

**3**

Use long multiplication to answer these calculations.

**a**    245 × 18

**b**    765 × 21

**c**    1356 × 23

**d**    2787 × 26

Use the written method for division to answer these calculations.

**e**    134 ÷ 5

**f**    256 ÷ 6

**g**    345 ÷ 8

**h**    986 ÷ 9

> **You need:**
> ● counters

> Make sure you show the remainders as fractions.

# Did you know?

The Ancient Egyptians did division by doubling. They would have answered 192 ÷ 8 like this:

| 1 | 8 |
| 2 | 16 |
| 4 | 32 |
| 8 | 64 |
| 16 | 128 |

128 + 16 = 144

16 + 2 = 18,
so 145 ÷ 8 = 18
REMAINDER 1

I can see from the table that 8 × 8 = 64 and 16 × 8 = 128. If I add the products I get 192. So 192 divided by 8 gives me 24 (16 + 8).

# Perimeter, area and volume

What do you have to measure to find the area of each tennis court?

How can you compare the size of these carpets?

I wonder how you can estimate the areas of these footprints?

How could you make a copy of this garden?

I wonder how much water is in the bottle and in the glass?

Teacher's Guide
Look at the pictures with the children and discuss the questions.
See pages 180–1 of the *Teacher's Guide* for key ideas to draw out.

167

**Let's learn**

I don't think we can work out the perimeter of a shape made up from rectangles unless we know the length of every side.

You're wrong! We can use the properties of a rectangle to work out the length of the missing sides.

**You need:**
- squared paper
- ruler
- trundle wheel
- tape measure

## Finding missing lengths

To find the perimeter of the rectilinear shape, find the length of each side. Next find the total length.

Opposite sides of a rectangle are equal in length. Use this property to find the missing lengths.

The total perimeter for this shape is 32 cm.

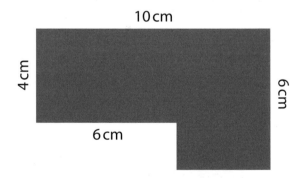

## Using a formula to find a perimeter

The perimeter (P) of a rectangle can be written as a formula with length (*l*) and width (*w*).

$$P = 2l + 2w \qquad \text{or} \qquad P = 2\,(l + w)$$

Use the formula to find the perimeter.

Use it to find the length if you know the perimeter and width, e.g. P = 28 cm, *l* = 10 cm, find the width.

Teacher's Guide

Before working through the *Textbook*, study page 182 of the *Teacher's Guide* to see how the concepts should be introduced. Read and discuss the page with the children. Provide concrete resources to support exploration.

**1**

## Answer these.

Find the perimeter of each polygon.

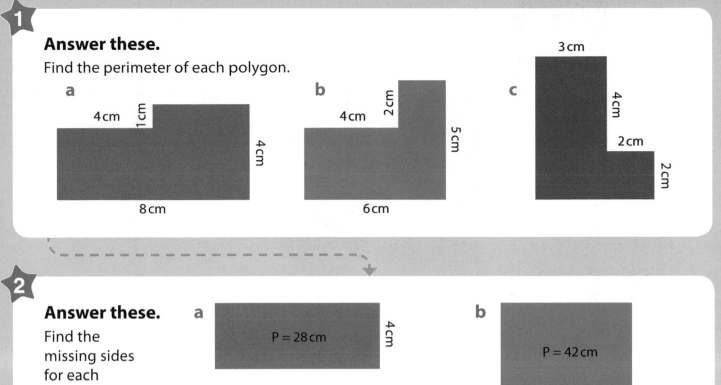

**a**
4 cm
1 cm
4 cm
8 cm

**b**
4 cm
2 cm
5 cm
6 cm

**c**
3 cm
4 cm
2 cm
2 cm

**2**

## Answer these.

Find the missing sides for each rectangle.

**a**
P = 28 cm
4 cm

**b**
P = 42 cm
12 cm

**c**
P = 42 cm
3 cm

**d** Find 3 different rectangles which have sides equal to a whole number of centimetres and a perimeter of 12 cm.

**3**

## Measure.

Choose a rectangular space somewhere outside your classroom, e.g. a patio or sports pitch.

Estimate the perimeter.

Decide what measurements you need to make to find the perimeter.

Use a tape measure or trundle wheel to find the measurements.

Record your results clearly.

**4**

## Investigate.

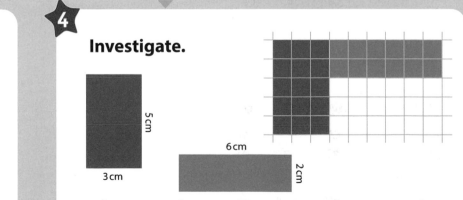

5 cm
3 cm
6 cm
2 cm

Using squared paper, draw and join the 2 rectangles in 4 different ways.

The sides must meet, not just touch at 2 vertices.

Predict which shape will have the largest and the smallest perimeter.

Work out the perimeter for each shape.

Were your predictions correct?

Teacher's Guide
See page 183 of the *Teacher's Guide* for ideas of how to guide practice. Work through each step together as a class to develop children's conceptual understanding.

**169** ★

Let's learn

You need:
- squared paper
- ruler
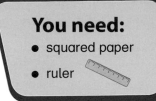

If the areas of two shapes are the same, their perimeters must be the same.

That's not right! They may have the same area, but that doesn't mean that they have to have the same perimeter.

## Finding area using a formula

Area is the amount of surface inside a perimeter.

There are 3 rows of 4 square centimetres.

Count the squares: 3 lots of 4 make 12, so the area is $12\,\text{cm}^2$.
The perimeter is 14 cm.

Imagine lines for squares on the second rectangle. You can count 2 rows of 6 squares. This also gives an area of $12\,\text{cm}^2$.
The perimeter is 16 cm.

The formula for area is:
$A = l \times w$ (A = area, $l$ = length and $w$ = width)

## Finding the area of irregular shapes

To find the area of a composite rectangular shape:

- divide it into rectangles
- find the area of each rectangle
- calculate the total.

The same shape can be divided in different ways:

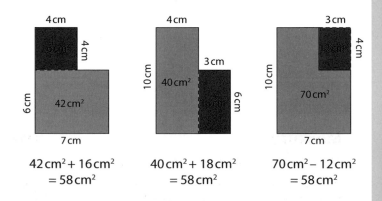

$42\,\text{cm}^2 + 16\,\text{cm}^2$ $= 58\,\text{cm}^2$

$40\,\text{cm}^2 + 18\,\text{cm}^2$ $= 58\,\text{cm}^2$

$70\,\text{cm}^2 - 12\,\text{cm}^2$ $= 58\,\text{cm}^2$

Each way gives the same answer.

In the third diagram the area of a rectangle larger than the shape is calculated. The area of the missing piece is then taken away.

Teacher's Guide

Before working through the *Textbook*, study page 184 of the *Teacher's Guide* to see how the concepts should be introduced. Read and discuss the page with the children. Provide concrete resources to support exploration.

**1**

## Answer these.

Find the area and perimeter.

**a** Find the area and perimeter of these shapes.

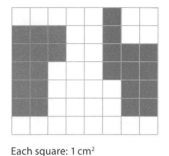

Each square: 1 cm²

**b** Draw 2 rectangular shapes with the same area but different perimeter lengths. Label the lengths of the sides. Show the perimeter and area.

**c** Estimate the area of this irregular shape.

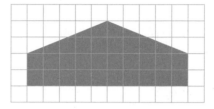

**2**

## Calculate.

Find the length of the missing sides in these rectangles. Calculate the perimeters.

**a** Area = 20 m²  Length of 1 side = 4 m

**b** Area = 24 m²  Length of 1 side = 8 m

**c** Area = 28 m²  Length of 1 side = 7 m

**d** A gardener digs a rectangular flowerbed at either end of his lawn. Draw a diagram showing the 2 flowerbeds.
Show the sizes of the flowerbeds.
What is the new area of lawn? What is the new perimeter?

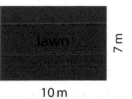

lawn

7 m

10 m

**3**

## Measure.

Measure the perimeter of these items. Calculate the top surface area. Work to the nearest whole centimetre.

**a** a book

**b** a pencil box

**c** another small item of your choice.

**4**

## Investigate.

A hexomino is a polygon made of 6 equal size squares connected edge to edge.

Make as many as you can.
Predict one with the largest and smallest perimeter.

Here is an allowable hexomino.

This one is not allowed.

Teacher's Guide
See page 185 of the *Teacher's Guide* for ideas of how to guide practice.
Work through each step together as a class to develop children's conceptual understanding.

171 ★

# Volume and capacity

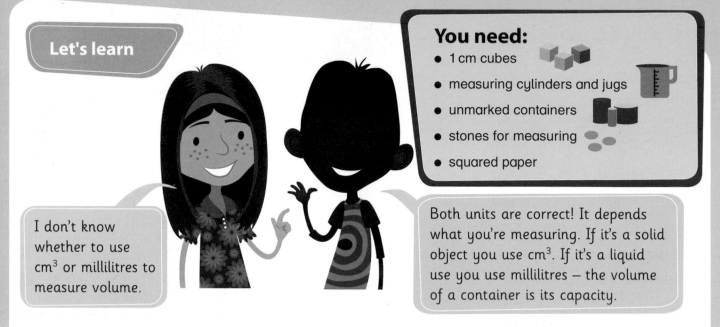

Let's learn

**You need:**
- 1 cm cubes
- measuring cylinders and jugs
- unmarked containers
- stones for measuring
- squared paper

I don't know whether to use cm³ or millilitres to measure volume.

Both units are correct! It depends what you're measuring. If it's a solid object you use cm³. If it's a liquid use you use millilitres – the volume of a container is its capacity.

## Volume and capacity – what's the difference?

**Volume** is the amount of space something takes up.

The volume of a solid object is measured in metres cubed (m³) or centimetres cubed (cm³).

To estimate the volume of a cuboid or cube, work out how many centimetre cubes would be needed to make it.

A cube with an edge of 2 cm, needs 8 × 1 cm cubes. The volume is 8 cm³.

**Capacity** is the amount a hollow 3-D container can hold. It is measured in millilitres or litres.
This 1 litre cube has 500 ml of water in it. The volume of water is 500 ml. The capacity of the cube is 1 litre.

## Volume of cuboids

These cuboids are made from 1 cm cubes.

Work out the volume of each cuboid. Count the number of cubes in each layer.

| | | |
|---|---|---|
| 8 cubes (volume = 8 cm³) | 16 cubes (volume = 16 cm³) | 24 cubes (volume = 24 cm³) |

Teacher's Guide

Before working through the *Textbook*, study page 186 of the *Teacher's Guide* to see how the concepts should be introduced. Read and discuss the page with the children. Provide concrete resources to support exploration.

## 1 Make.

Make some cuboids.

Complete each shape to make the smallest possible cuboid.

How many cubes are there in each cuboid?

Estimate the volume of each shape.

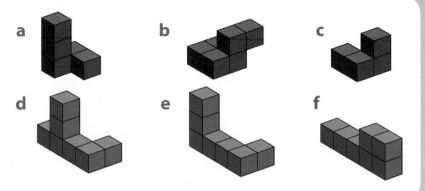

## 2 Measure.

Find the capacity.

Choose 6 containers.

Put them in order of increasing capacity.

Estimate the capacity of each.

Fill each with water to find its actual capacity in millilitres.

Record your results in a table.

| Container | Description or sketch | Estimate of capacity | Actual capacity |
|-----------|----------------------|---------------------|-----------------|
| 1 | | | |
| 2 | | | |
| etc. | | | |

Was your order correct?
Did your estimates improve?

## 3 Experiment.

Fill a 1 litre measuring jug with 500 ml of water.

Slide a stone into the water. Do not splash.

Read the new volume of water.

The stone has increased the reading by its own volume.

Find the difference in the 2 readings in millilitres.

The number of millilitres is equal to the volume of the stone in cm³ because 1 ml of water takes up 1 cm³ space.

Record your results.

## 4 Investigate.

Cut out a 10 cm × 10 cm square from squared paper. Fold along the dotted lines. Cut a 1 cm square from each corner. Fold the edges up to make an open box.

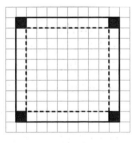

How many centimetre cubes can you fit in the box? Would this be its volume or its capacity?

Cut out another 10 cm × 10 cm square. Cut a 2 cm × 2 cm square from each corner.

How many cubes can you fit in this box?

Cut different size squares from the corners.

Which box holds the most cubes?

Record your results.

Teacher's Guide

See page 187 of the *Teacher's Guide* for ideas of how to guide practice. Work through each step together as a class to develop children's conceptual understanding.

173

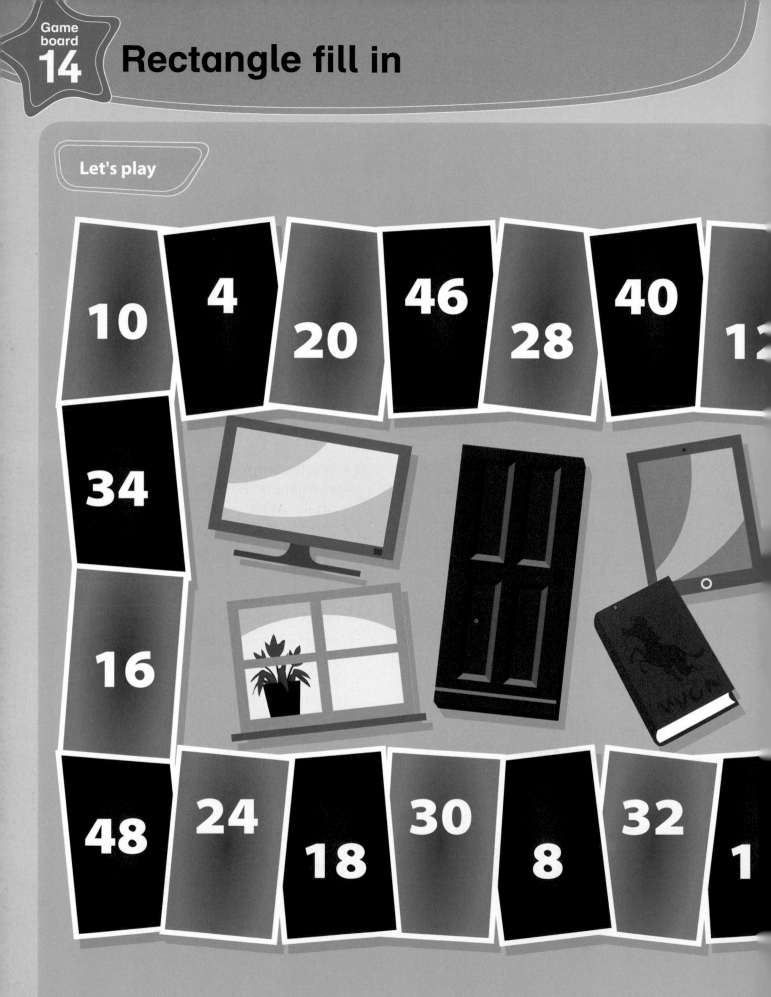

Let's play

10

4

20

46

28

40

12

34

16

48

24

18

30

8

32

1

Teacher's Guide

See pages 188–9 of the *Teacher's Guide*. Explain the rules for each game and allow children to choose which to play. Encourage them to challenge themselves and practise what they have learnt in the unit.

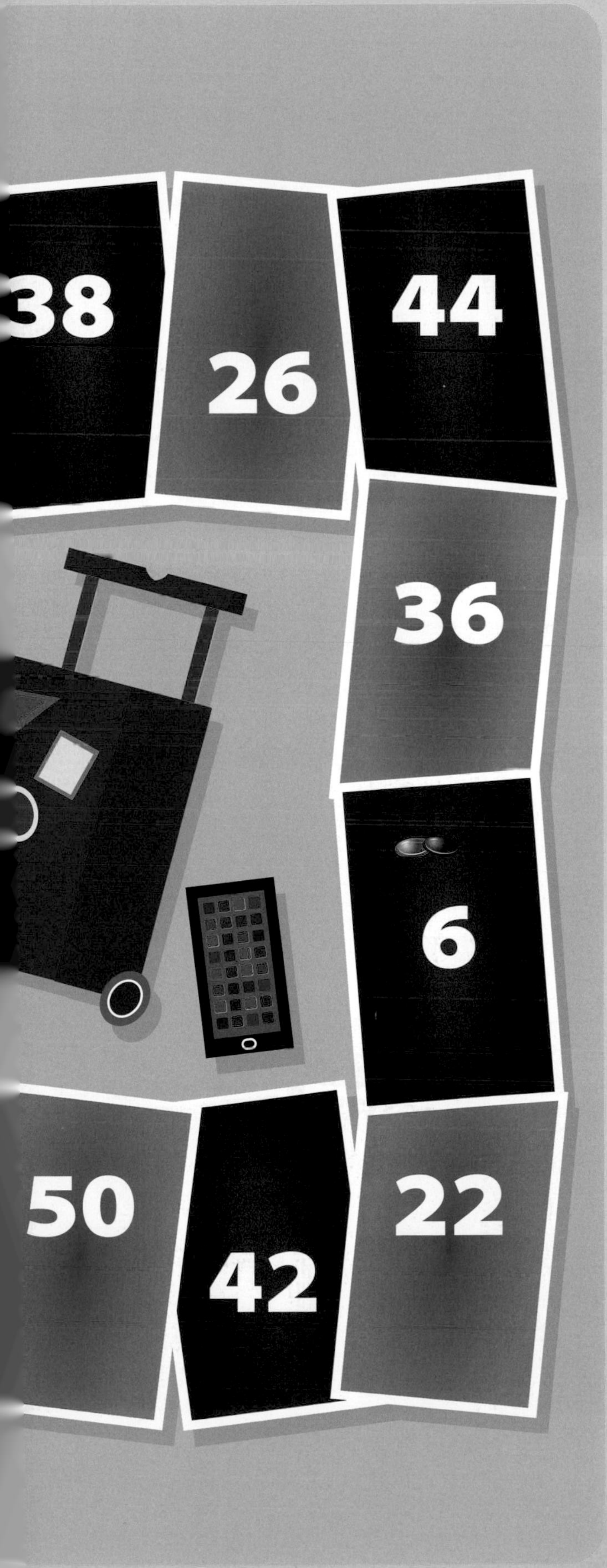

38
26
44
36
6
50
42
22

**You need:**

- large sheet of squared paper
- 1–6 dice
- red and blue counters
- red and blue pencils

### 1 Perimeter challenge

Choose your perimeter and fill a grid with rectangles. Who will be able to make the most?

### 2 Area challenge

Choose your area and fill a grid with rectangles. Who will be able to make the most?

### 3 Your game

Design your own game.

Explain the rules and play with a partner.

# And finally ...

**Let's review**

**1**

Here are 2 patios. Calculate the area of each patio in 2 different ways. Explain how you did it.

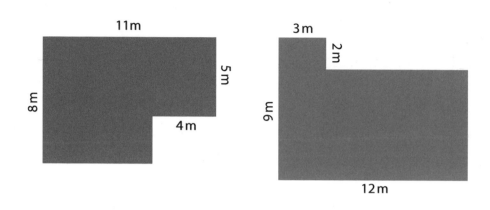

**2**

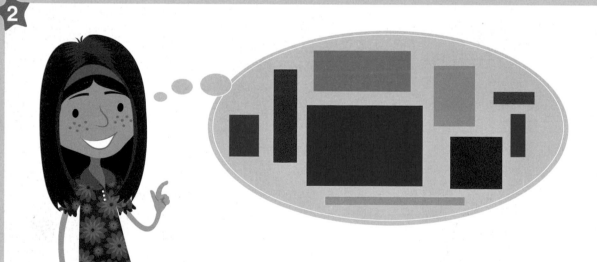

Find some rectangles where:

- the perimeter is numerically greater than the area
- the area is numerically greater than the perimeter.

Find one or more rectangles where:

- the perimeter and area are numerically equal.

Have you found any relationship in rectangles between perimeter, area and size?

Teacher's Guide

See pages 190–1 of the *Teacher's Guide* for guidance on running each task. Observe children to identify those who have mastered concepts and those who require further consolidation.

**3** Your teacher will show you some items like the ones below.
Estimate their capacity. You can choose whether to use litres or millilitres.

| can of fizzy drink | washing-up bowl | squash bottle | mug |
| bucket | juice carton | kettle | teaspoon |

# Did you know?

A Greek legend says that Queen Dido founded the ancient city of Carthage. She and some of her people were camped on Byrsa Hill, which overlooks the land and sea. The local chief told them they could have as much land as could be enveloped by a single ox hide.

Yes, and clever Dido cut the ox hide into thin strips and placed them on the ground end to end until she had completely encircled Byrsa Hill!

## 2-dimensional (2-D)

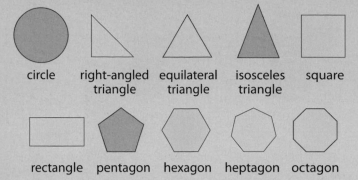

circle | right-angled triangle | equilateral triangle | isosceles triangle | square

rectangle | pentagon | hexagon | heptagon | octagon

## 3-dimensional (3-D)

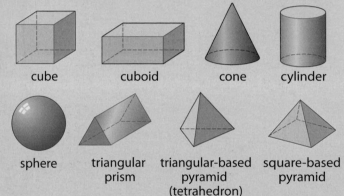

cube | cuboid | cone | cylinder

sphere | triangular prism | triangular-based pyramid (tetrahedron) | square-based pyramid

## A

### addend

The number being added in an addition calculation.
Augend + addend = sum (or total). See also *augend*.

$$3 + 5 = 8$$
augend   addend   sum/total

### array

An arrangement of numbers, shapes or objects in rows of equal size and columns of equal size, used to find out how many altogether.

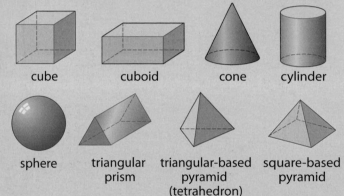
column
row →

$12 \times 3 = 36$

### ascending/descending order

Ascending order: putting values in order from smallest to largest. Descending order: putting values in order from largest to smallest.

### augend

The number being added to is in an addition calculation.
Augend + addend = sum (or total).

$$3 + 5 = 8$$
augend   addend   sum/total

### axis of symmetry

An axis of symmetry divides the shape into 2 identical parts. Also called a mirror line.

## B

### balance

Things are balanced when both sides have equal value, e.g. $3 + 4 = 2 + 5$ and $1000\,g = 1\,kg$.

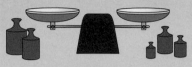

### bar line chart

A statistical diagram using lines to show the frequency of discrete outcomes.

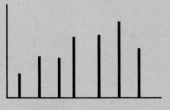

## C

### capacity

The amount a container holds. It is measured in litres or millilitres, e.g. the capacity of a 2 litre bottle is 2 litres.

### Celsius

A scale used to measure temperature. Sometimes called Centigrade. Units are °C.

### commutative

Addition and multiplication are commutative. It doesn't matter which order you add or multiply, the answer is always the same. Same answer, different calculation, e.g. $3 + 4 = 4 + 3$. But subtraction is not commutative, e.g. $7 - 2 \neq 2 - 7$.

### composite number

A number that is not a prime number.

### concentric

Circles which share the same centre.

### congruent

Shapes are congruent if they are exactly the same shape and size.

### consecutive

Numbers which follow each other in order.

**13, 14, 15**
consecutive numbers

**24, 26, 28**
consecutive even numbers

### coordinate

An ordered pair of $(x, y)$ values that gives the position of a point on a graph. In 3-D $(x, y, z)$.

## cube number

Formed when a number is multiplied by itself and then by itself again, e.g.
2 cubed = $2 \times 2 \times 2 = 2^3 = 8$.

## cubic millimetres (mm³), cubic centimetres (cm³), cubic metres (m³), cubic kilometres (km³)

Metric measurements of liquid and solid volume. 1 cm³ is the volume enclosed in a cube of length 1 cm.

## currency

A money system. In the UK, the currency is the pounds stirling (£). In the EU, the currency is the Euro (€).

# D

## data

Numbers collected from a questionnaire or survey.

## denominator

The number underneath the vinculum. Also called the divisor.

## difference

The result of a subtraction. The difference between 12 and 5 is 7. See also *minuend, subtrahend*.

## digit total/sum

The sum of all the digits in a number,
e.g. the digit sum of 435 is 4 + 3 + 5 = 12, and 1 + 2 = 3.

## discount

A reduction offered on the price of an item for sale

## dividend

The number that is divided in a division sum. See also *divisor, quotient, division bracket*.

dividend
↓
$12 \div 6 = 2$ ← quotient
↑
divisor

## divisibility

Whether a number can be divided without remainder. All even numbers are divisible by 2.

## division bracket

The half box around the dividend in a division. See also *dividend*.

$16\,)\overline{2112}$ ← dividend
↑
division bracket

## divisor

The number used to divide in a division sum,
e.g. in 12 ÷ 6 = 2, 6 is the divisor. See also *dividend, quotient*.

# E

## equilateral triangle

A triangle with three equal sides and three equal angles of 60°.

## equivalent

Two numbers or expressions that are equal, but which can be in a different form, e.g. £1 is equivalent to 100p. Two fractions are equivalent if they have the same value, e.g $\frac{2}{6} = \frac{1}{3}$.

# F

## factor

Numbers that divide exactly into a number are its factors, e.g. the factors of 12 are 1, 2, 3, 4, 6, 12.

## factor pair

Two factors that multiply together to give the number, e.g. the factor pairs of 12 are 1 × 12, 2 × 6, 3 × 4.

## formula, formulae

A mathematical statement using letters or symbols (variables), e.g. Area of a rectangle = length × width or A = $l \times w$.

# G

## gallon

An imperial measure of capacity. 1 gallon is approximately 4.5 litres. See also *pint*.

## greater than or equal to

Symbol: ≥. An inequality showing the lowest value a number can take. $n \geq 7$ means $n$ can have any value from 7 upwards. See also *less than or equal to*.

# I

## imperial unit

A non-metric unit of measure, e.g. inches, yards, miles, pints. Many are still in common use.

## in every, for every

A way of expressing proportion (in every) and ratio (for every), e.g. one in every ten pupils has a dog and there are three apples for every four bananas in the fruit salad recipe.

## integer, positive, negative

An integer is a whole number which can be positive or negative, e.g. -4, -2, 4, 100.

## isosceles triangle

A triangle with two equal sides and two equal base angles.
One of its angles can be a right angle.
This is called a right-angled isosceles triangle.

# K

## kite

A quadrilateral with two pairs of equal sides.

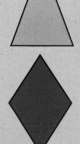

# L

## least popular, least common

In statistics. The value or outcome that happens least often. See also *most popular, most common*.

### less than or equal to

Symbol: ≤. An inequality showing the highest value a number can take. $n \leq 7$ means $n$ can have any value up to and including 7. See also *greater than or equal to*.

### line

A line is straight. It has no thickness and extends in both directions without ending.

### line graph

A graph with a continuous line showing the trend or variation in a value.

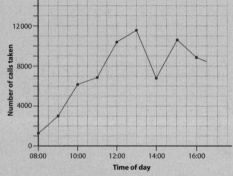

## M

### mass

A measure of the amount of matter in an object. Measured in grams (g), kilograms (kg) or tonnes (t).

### maximum/minimum value

The largest/smallest value a number or variable can take.

### metric unit

Any unit used to measure using a metric scale, e.g. kilograms, centimetres, litres. All are based on the decimal system.

### minuend

The starting number in a subtraction calculation, e.g. 10 (the minuend) – 3 (the subtrahend) = 7 (the difference). See also *subtrahend* and *difference*.

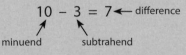

### mixed number

A number with both a whole number part and a fractional part, e.g. $3\frac{1}{2}$.

### most popular, most common

In statistics. The most frequently occurring outcome. See also *least popular, least common*.

### multiple

A multiple is the product of two numbers, e.g. the multiples of 7 are 7, 14, 21, 28, etc.

### multiplicand

A number to be multiplied, e.g. in $6 \times 3 = 18$, 6 is the multiplicand. See also *multiplier* and *product*.

$$6 \times 3 = 18 \leftarrow \text{product}$$
$$\underset{\text{multiplicand}}{\uparrow} \qquad \underset{\text{multiplier}}{\uparrow}$$

### multiplier

The multiplying number, e.g. in $6 \times 3 = 18$, 3 is the multiplier. See also *multiplicand* and *product*.

## N

### numerator

The number above the vinculum in a fraction. See also *denominator*.

## O

### octahedron

A 3-D shape with 8 triangular faces.

### ones boundary

When counting from a decimal to a whole number, the ones boundary is crossed. See also *tenths boundary*.

### outcome

One of the possible results from a statistical experiment or trial. E.g. when tossing a coin there are two equally-likely outcomes: heads or tails.

## P

### parallelogram

A 2-D shape with two pairs of opposite sides that are equal and parallel. A rectangle is a parallelogram with all the angles 90°.

### percentage, per cent, %

A fraction expressed as a part of a hundred, e.g. $\frac{1}{2} = \frac{5}{100} = 50\%$.

### pint

An imperial measure of capacity. There are 8 pints in a gallon. 1 litre is approximately 1.75 pints.

### prime number

A number with only two factors, itself and 1. 1 is NOT a prime number.

### product

The result of multiplying two numbers. The product of 4 and 3 is $4 \times 3 = 12$.

$$4 \times 3 = 12 \leftarrow \text{product}$$
$$\underset{\text{multiplicand}}{\uparrow} \qquad \underset{\text{multiplier}}{\uparrow}$$

### proper/improper fraction

In an improper fraction, the numerator is larger than the denominator, e.g. $\frac{5}{2}$. In a proper fraction the denominator is larger.

## Q

### quadrant

One of the four quarters formed by the $x$- and $y$-axes on a graph.

### quadrilateral

A 2-D shape with four straight sides.

### quotient

The answer to a division calculation, e.g. in $12 \div 6 = 2$, 2 is the quotient. See also *dividend*.

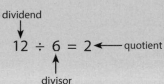

## R

### radius

Any straight line segment from the centre of a circle to the edge (circumference). The radius is half of the diameter.

### reduced to, simplify

To reduce or simplify a fraction, divide both numbers by the highest common factor, e.g. $\frac{6}{9} = \frac{2}{3}$.

### reflective symmetry

A figure or object has reflective symmetry if there is a line (2-D) or a plane (3-D) which can divide the shape into 2 identical parts.

line of symmetry

### reflex angle

An angle greater than 180°.

### rhombus

A 2-D shape with four equal sides, no right-angles and equal opposite angles.

## S

### scalene triangle

A triangle with no equal sides or angles. A scalene triangle can have a right angle. This is called a right-angled scalene triangle.

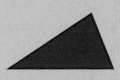

### square millimetre (mm²), square centimetre (cm²), square metre (m²)

Metric units of measure of area equivalent to a square 1 mm × 1 mm, 1 cm × 1 cm or 1 m × 1 m. Symbol: mm², cm² and m².

### square number

The square numbers are a sequence $1^2$, $2^2$, $3^2$, formed by multiplying each number by itself. This gives the numbers 1, 4, 9, 16, 25 and so on. See also *cube number*.

### subtrahend

The number that is subtracted from the minuend.

### sum

The answer to an addition calculation. The sum of 4 and 5 is 9. See also *total*.

### surface

The face or faces of a 3-D shape.

## T

### ten thousand

10 000.

### tenths boundary

When counting from a hundredth to a tenth, the tenths boundary is crossed. See also *ones boundary*.

### thousandths

$\frac{1}{1000} = 0.001$.

### total

The answer to an addition calculation. The total of 4, 3 and 5 is 12. See also *sum*.

### trapezium

A quadrilateral with 1 pair of parallel sides.

## V

### vinculum

The line that separates the numerator and denominator in a fraction.

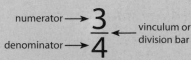

### volume

The amount of liquid in a container, e.g. 1 litre of water in a 2 l bottle. Measured in millilitres and litres. See also *capacity*.

# W

### weight

The force exerted on a mass by gravity. The units are units of force (Newtons). Often confused with mass.

### whole-part relationship

Parts of the whole. In the fraction $\frac{2}{3}$, the whole has been divided into three equal parts and we are thinking about two of those parts.

# X

### *x*-axis

The horizontal line on a graph or coordinate grid that runs through zero.

# Y

### *y*-axis

The vertical line on a graph or coordinate grid that runs through zero.